Pelican Books

Indonesia Since

Born at Streaky Bay, South Australia, in 1934,
Peter Polomka has had extensive experience
reporting Southeast Asian affairs. After graduating
bachelor of agricultural science from Adelaide
University in 1955, he worked on the Adelaide
Advertiser and Melbourne *Herald* before joining the
Straits Times, Malaya, early in 1963. During 1964
and 1965, he was managing editor of the *Bangkok Post*,
Thailand, and from 1966 until late in 1968, resident
correspondent in Indonesia for the Melbourne
Herald/Sun, and a special correspondent for the
Washington *Post*. He is also a graduate of Melbourne
University, and qualified for the degree of master of
arts with a thesis on Indonesian foreign policy.

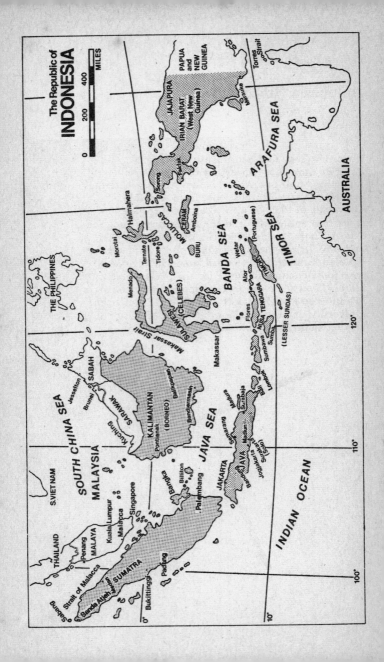

Peter Polomka

Indonesia Since Sukarno

Penguin Books

Penguin Books Ltd, Harmondsworth,
Middlesex, England

Penguin Books Australia Ltd, Ringwood,
Victoria, Australia

First published 1971
Copyright © Peter Polomka, 1971

Printed in Australia for
Penguin Books Australia Ltd,
at The Dominion Press, Blackburn, Victoria
Set in Lintoype Baskerville

Contents

Introduction

On 1 October 1965, an attempted *coup d'état* led by left-wing and communist forces plunged Indonesia into violent conflict. By early 1966, perhaps more than 300,000 people lay dead, victims of the fury unleashed as the anti-communists, led by the Indonesian National Army (TNI), ruthlessly set about annihilating the Indonesian Communist Party (PKI). At the same time, the leadership of President Sukarno – the nation's most illustrious son – came under increasingly sharp attack, until in March 1966 he was forced to cede important emergency powers to the commander of the army, General Suharto. In the protracted struggle that ensued, with Suharto and Sukarno as focal points of opposing political forces, Sukarno's authority continued to decline until in February 1967 he signed over his remaining powers to Suharto. The following month, a full session of Congress (MPRS), the country's supreme constitutional authority, formally stripped President Sukarno of all powers of office and appointed General Suharto Acting President, pending the holding of national elections. In March 1968, a further session of Congress elevated Suharto to the position of full President for a five year term. In June 1970, Sukarno died, and was buried at Blitar, East Java, with state honours.

Today, with an exploding population already exceeding 120 million, Indonesia ranks after China, India, the Soviet Union and the United States as the fifth most populous state in the world. It is also among the most complex. Its people encompass more than 300 ethnic groups and over 250 distinct languages. They range from sophisticated city dwellers to semi-nomadic jungle people, scarcely emerged from the Stone Age. There are people operating complex computers; others unable to cope fully with the wheel. Some worship the modern gods of Marx and Lenin; others the enduring spirits of their own ancestors. Some espouse modern doctrines on government and the rights of man; others take refuge in ancient customs and tribal laws.

Bhinneka Tunggal Ika – Unity in Diversity – is the proud motto of the Republic of Indonesia. It remains more an aspiration than a reality. Already the people have tried and abandoned two systems of government – a hybrid of Western parliamentary democracy in the fifties and the so-called Guided Democracy in the sixties. Gropingly, they now seek a third, more effective system, capable of accommodating and reconciling the country's diversity while still coping with the day-to-day problems of government.

Before the October 1965 attempted *coup*, Indonesia constantly captured world headlines as Sukarno pursued what he grandly called his 'global strategy' for 'building the world anew'. Since the *coup*, the country has turned inward to concentrate on repairing the ravages of Sukarno's economic misrule, and, as a result, has slipped from world notoriety. But its significance among the community of nations has scarcely declined. With Western military power in retreat from its bridgeheads in Southeast Asia, the development of a cohesive, stable Indonesia may not only be the best hope for the peace and security of the region; it may be the only hope.

But what of that hope? During a state address in August 1970 commemorating the twenty-fifth anniversary of the Republic, President Suharto touched on what, perhaps, is the heart of the problem:

Only part of us — just the smaller part — has enjoyed the fruits of independence. The greater part however — soldiers, civil servants, small peasants and labourers — still live a difficult life. They still live in inadequate houses in alleys and dirty slums without fresh drinking water and without electricity, with a low degree of nutrition, deeply concerned about the schooling and education of their children — as if looking forward into a dark future.[1]

Will the future grow darker as the seventies advance? Or can the country's present leadership succeed where Sukarno failed? These are questions the following chapters attempt to answer as they explore the country's complexity, the reasons for the failure of Guided Democracy, the rise of the army to power, the kind of leadership and policies Suharto has brought to the Republic in the post-*coup* period, the forbidding political, economic, social and religious problems his administration confronts, and the Indonesian people's continued search for unity from amid their diversity.

1. 'Address of State delivered by the President of the Republic of Indonesia, before the House of Representatives on the eve of the 25th Independence Day, on 16 August 1970', Department of Information, Jakarta, p. 3.

Chapter 1

The Dream and the Reality

Night has fallen on the Central Javanese village of Wedi. The people are gathered – the young and the old. They wait patiently, watching a man who is sitting cross-legged beneath a large, suspended oil lamp, and facing a taut white screen. Suddenly, he raps for silence, intones some prayers, and in a deep, resonant voice begins:

Long, long ago there was a vast country called Kosala, which was known far and wide as a great, glorious land. Its soil was very rich; its plains were so fertile anything would grow, and grow well. Nor was there any shortage of water. It is therefore no wonder that crops always gave good harvests. Food and clothes were very cheap. Everyone was well dressed; everyone was well fed. In all Kosala, there was not a single thief. In fact, the thought of theft never entered anybody's head. Cows, horses and other domestic animals were never tied up at night; they just moved about freely at all times. The climate was good all the year round. *Gotong rojong*, or helping each other, was strong among the people. They were polite and kind to each other, as well as to strangers. Food and shelter for the night awaited the tired traveller who happened to knock at anybody's door . . .

As his hypnotic voice continues, his hands are never still, recreating the kingdom of Kosala with deft movements of bizarre, leather puppets that cast their shadows across the screen. Soon his audience is lost in reverie, swept along by the melody and rhythm of the gamelan music blending in the background. Carefree, they wander in a dream world peopled with gods, kings, priests, princesses, warriors, giants, buffoons, birds and apes. At least until the breaking dawn brings this version of the Ramayana story to a close, the people of Wedi are freed from their daily concerns, and full of hope for life in an Indonesian 'Kosala' of the future.

But there is another story from the Indonesian 'Kosala' of the immediate past. It is told not by puppeteers of traditional shadow theatre *(wajang)* but by economists writing in the introductory chapter of the national Five-Year Development Plan begun in April 1969. It begins on a less tranquil note:

During the last decades, the economy was the servant of politics. Rational economic principles were ignored. Domestic and foreign resources were squandered. The direct result was a decline in the economy accompanied by hyperinflation, which became more and more critical. Shortages were felt in many sectors, such as food, textiles, tools for production, spare parts, raw materials, etc. The irrigation system, plantations, mines, factories, road networks, electricity, drinking water, railways, airports, harbours and telecommunication facilities were virtually neglected.

Food production did not keep pace with population growth. Export proceeds decreased significantly, while imports were paid for by ever increasing loans from abroad.

Employment opportunities became fewer, as the economy declined. The only field of work which always expanded was government service. The increasing number of civil servants pushed up routine expenses. However, revenues available in real value were not proportional to the number of people employed, so that the real income of civil servants declined.

Consequently, the rate of economic growth during the last decades was very low, especially when it is compared with the rate of population increase, so that in reality the income of the people per capita dwindled or was stagnant. As a result, various social facilities were neglected. Those for education, health, recreation, religion, etc., were not able to keep pace with demand The development of education was not in line with the development of the economy, with the result that graduates were jobless.

All this created an atmosphere of despair, apathy, loss of interest, and a spirit of indifference. All walks of life were affected by lethargy, disappointment and frustration . . . [1]

The dream and the reality; the aspiration and experience – not just of the people of Wedi, but of a nation. For although Indonesian national policy does not mention Kosala by name, the 'just and prosperous' society that the Republic has promised its citizens since gaining independence from Dutch colonial rule more than two decades ago bears a striking similarity to the 'great, glorious land' of the Ramayana legend. To achieve such a society, the 1945 Constitution of the Republic of Indonesia stipulates that the economy 'shall be organized as a common endeavour based upon the principle of the family system'; that 'branches of production which are important for the state and which affect the life of most people shall be controlled by the state and made use of for the people'; and that the 'poor, and destitute children, shall be cared for by the state'. Few would argue with such creditable aims, nor deny how far they are from fulfilment in Indonesia. Yet even today, one constantly encounters an air of unreality about economic matters within the country.

Perhaps too many Indonesians have come to believe the repetitive propaganda of their first president, Sukarno, about the archipelago's proverbial riches. Indonesia, he often asserted, could comfortably support 250 million people. And he may eventually be proved right – but not on the record of the first two decades of independence. For centuries, the country has been famed for its quality tropical produce – spices from the Moluccas, pepper and rubber from Sumatra, and the famous Java coffees and teas. At various times, it has been among the world's foremost producers of sugar, rubber, coffee, tea, tobacco and other crops. But its rich agricultural lands are not unlimited, despite what many Indonesians might think. The highly

1. *The First Five-Year Development Plan (1969–70 – 1973–4)*, vol. 1, Department of Information, Jakarta, p. 8.

fertile soils are confined to a few regions of volcanic activity in Java, Bali, Lombok, parts of Sumatra and Sulawesi (Celebes), and some of these lands in Java are already the most densely populated agricultural areas in the world. All too often in Indonesia, the luxuriant looking canopy of impenetrable jungle still covering many of the islands hides infertile soils. And much of the country's legendary mineral wealth still has to be discovered. Rich deposits of oil, tin, nickel and other minerals have already been tapped, but known reserves are far from inexhaustible, and until the recent arrival of foreign prospectors, little or nothing had been done by way of survey work since the days of the Dutch. Likewise, there has been a singular lack of economic endeavour in so many other fields.

Perhaps too many Indonesians have been excessively influenced by the 'golden' promises of their political leaders. Sukarno admitted some of his people thought that with *merdeka* – as 'freedom' or 'independence' was called – they would no longer be expected to pay for things like bus or train fares – all would be free. And it was a misguided belief Sukarno personally did little to dispel. Under Guided Democracy, during the years preceding the attempted *coup*, such was the feather-bedding of city dwellers they payed little or nothing for reticulated water, electricity, and other government services. Plane, bus and train fares were probably the cheapest in the world. Petrol was less costly than tea. Of course, all this was heavily subsidized by the government, partly by borrowing money from abroad since it was more than the country's economy could afford. Even so, it amounted to no more than what the average city dweller had come to expect as his due.

Perhaps the air of unreality about economic matters is also related to the fact that few Indonesian leaders have ever had to earn a living with their hands. It is strange listening to government officials telling village people they must work harder. In Java, they have even enlisted the aid of puppeteers for this purpose. A celebrated puppeteer in Central Java, Ki Raden Sunartosabdho, told me in 1969 he was co-operating with the administration by, among other things, telling farmers they should extend their working day from 7 a.m. to 7 p.m., instead of finishing work at 2 p.m. In contrast, thousands of government officials barely work from 9 a.m. to 12 p.m. (although their office hours are nominally from 7.30 a.m. to 2 p.m.), and spend much of this period sipping coffee, chatting, and scanning the morning papers. And yet some city dwellers even lay the blame for their country's economic failings at the feet of the 'lazy peasants'.

But whatever the reasons, there is little correlation in Indonesia between hard work and wealth. All too often one finds the attitude that only the dull, stupid and socially inferior dirty their hands. And the worst example is often given right at the top where many seek instant fortunes through shady business deals, corruption, and exploiting their proximity to the seat of power. Lower down the rung, countless able, well qualified people prefer to live on their wits – looking for the quick, easy commission – rather than settle for a more useful, regular job. This is not to suggest that all city dwellers are idle and unproductive. They are not, and many work hard at legitimate jobs. But all too often, hard work earns too little recognition, while the slick operator wins approval as he makes his already luxurious home more luxurious, and adds another Mercedes to his stable of cars.

Many Indonesians also do not appear to recognize the extent to which their farmers subsidize life in the cities. Instead, they frequently complain that peasants rarely pay taxes. But some indication of the real situation can be found in the sums the national rice buying agency, BULOG, pays for its local purchases, compared with the cost of rice imported from abroad. For instance, during its 1970–1971 procurement programme, BULOG expected to buy more than 600,000 tons of rice from Indonesian farmers at about half the cost of a similar quantity purchased from abroad. And even then, there is no guarantee that the farmer will get the minimum price to which he is entitled since BULOG buys through middle-men who are adept at squeezing powerless peasants. Nor can the farmer sell part of his harvest at higher prices, since BULOG functions partly as a price control agency to prevent the price of the country's basic foodstuff sky-rocketing in politically sensitive urban communities. Likewise, through countless other practices, farmers get only a fraction of world prices for most of their produce. They are also often expected to pay inflated prices for fertilizers and other needs. And this is under the new post-*coup* administration that has declared itself genuinely committed to giving the farmer a 'new deal'.

Under Guided Democracy, the Indonesian village captured the attention of national ideologues. It was seized upon as the essence of everything that was truly 'Indonesian'. *Musjawarat* (consultations or discussion), *mupakat* (agreement), *gotong rojong* (mutual co-operation) – the ideological underpinnings of Indonesian society were all rediscovered amid the bamboo huts and earth floors of the traditional village, and recognized by Sukarno as the 'treasury of the Indonesian people which has lain buried during hundreds of years of foreign rule'. 'You must be aware that the village is in fact the source of our national identity,' a prominent government leader told a gathering of village heads in May 1964. 'Therefore the village is the centre of the growth of our national policy, culture and economy.' Little wonder if the average city dweller may have lost sight of the poverty and squalor that is often also associated with the traditional village in more modern times, and instead began regarding the peasants' lot as one of undisturbed harmony and bucolic bliss! And if the blood-bath in over-populated rural regions that followed the attempted *coup* has not erased that notion, what ever will?

Until quite recently, not many Indonesian leaders have run the risk of shattering their illusions concerning life in out-of-the-way rural areas. Few have cared to forsake their comfortable brick and concrete houses and kapok mattresses to share a makeshift bamboo bench with a struggling squatter and find out for themselves what country life can be like. I once visited a small, potentially prosperous town in South Sumatra that could recall only one fleeting visit by a cabinet minister in the past fifteen years – and this was a commercial centre for about 250,000 people, less than 500 miles from the Indonesian capital of Jakarta. Before independence, it was a thriving town, but had since slowly strangled as its links with the outside world – a nearby port and two roads – gradually slipped into disrepair and eventually became unusable. And this was not an isolated instance of government neglect, but the fate of hundreds of important rural centres scattered throughout the archipelago. And when government officials do travel from the comparative comfort of the capital, it is often with such pomp, ceremony and expense, that their illusions may well be confirmed.

Even so, there is really no need to travel beyond the major towns to recognize the plight of rural people since the poor and jobless flock to these places seeking food and work. In Jakarta, these refugees of national mismanagement number scores of thousands. And thousands more can be found in other major cities, such as Surabaja in East Java, and Medan in North Sumatra. In Jakarta, some find a hand-to-mouth existence pushing pedi-cabs by day and sleeping in them by night. Others get part time, menial work. But mostly they are forced to beg or steal, and camp in the open along the banks of the city's muddy, sewer-like canals. On occasions, such as the imminent arrival of a distinguished foreign visitor, those squatting among the more affluent suburbs have been known to be herded into trucks and dumped on the outskirts of the city. During more recent years, the city administration has been discouraging their presence by erecting miles of formidable, barbed-wire fence around the canals and parks they commonly frequent.

Admittedly, where economic and developmental problems are involved, Indonesian leaders labour under some especially unenviable legacies – though these are partly of their own making. Everything, it seems, must await 'government' action. Few, if anyone, can ever be found taking the initiative and trying to solve their own economic problems. Rarely, for instance, does one find the much praised system of *gotong rojong* (mutual co-operation) working spontaneously to repair roads, irrigation canals, and other infra-structure vital for maintaining and increasing production. Either military or government officials must get such operations underway, and it seems, there is no limit to the patience of the average Indonesian waiting for this to happen. Also, one man's misfortune is invariably another man's gain. When roads are no longer passable by truck (although a few hours work a week by the local people may have avoided their closure), others pushing bicycles and carrying loads upon their backs begin to make a profit. Of course, supplies run short, prices rise, and production is affected – but few seem really concerned about that. I once found rice trucks banked up at a broken bridge. A few men with axes could easily have wandered into the nearby forest, cut some suitable timber, and quickly repaired the bridge. Instead, rice was being carried sack by sack across the bridge to trucks waiting on the other side. It meant employment for a few more people, but also lower rice prices to local farmers and increased costs for the consumers. And if one retells stories such as these to Indonesian leaders in the cities, they mostly just shrug their shoulders. Some even get quite upset that a foreigner should make such impolite observations.

Many reasons are given for the average Indonesian's lack of initiative and foresight in economic affairs. Some blame the climate, others their colonial past. A few dig deeper into the paternal nature of traditional society, and the distaste with which the ancient aristocracy viewed money matters. Still others discern a strongly fatalistic streak that lives only for the present, fearing the possible rapacity of an unpredictable tomorrow. Whatever the cause, peasants often quickly spend their profits on parties, transistor radios and other odds-and-ends, even though they know that tomorrow they may be forced to borrow money at usurious interest rates in order to survive until the next harvest. And the average Indonesian businessman seems more concerned with get-rich-quick schemes and the appearances of affluence – a big house and a fine car – than with developing and maintaining a solid enterprise on a sound financial footing. Most of the foreign assets seized during the pre-*coup* years as Indonesia 'confronted' Malaysia quickly ran into the 'red' through reckless and incompetent management, and, when returned to their owners following the *coup*, were almost just as speedily returned to profitability. In North Sumatra, for instance, foreign interests resuming control of agricultural estates found impossible numbers of idle employees in administrative offices while the ranks of field labourers were often under strength. In many cases, this alone meant the difference between the plantation running at a profit or a loss.

*

What then of the future? Under President Suharto, the national administration has placed primary stress not only on rehabilitating and developing the country's economy, but also has focused its efforts especially on the agricultural sector. Since more than 75 per cent of the population gain their livelihood from the land, producing 55 per cent of the gross national product, and more than 60 per cent of the country's export income, there are sound economic and political reasons for choosing such a course. The Five-Year Development Plan states the broad strategy in these terms:

The aim is to carry out developmental efforts which will make possible a process of modernization directed towards breaking through the wall of economic backwardness, with targets concentrated in agricultural development. With agriculture as a starting point, developmental efforts in industry, mining, infra-structure, manpower, education, regional development and other sectors will be expanded.[1]

But does this necessarily mean the beginnings of a new era for Indonesian farmers? Has the 'message of the people's suffering' – a slogan popularized as Sukarno continued to squander the country's resources – finally got through to the Indonesian capital? While it is far too soon to give a categorical answer to such questions, not all the early signs are especially encouraging.

There are reasons for doubting the depth of the government commitment to agricultural reform. Among those who harbour these doubts is an Australian economist, David Penny, who has a close association with Indonesia dating back more than a decade. He believes contemporary Indonesian society retains many characteristics of the ancient Javanese agrarian empires, such as the Mataram and Madjapahit, that flourished from the eighth to the fifteenth century. These built imposing civilizations largely upon the labours of peasant farmers, and were noted for the paternal attitude of their rulers towards the people. Penny doubts whether relationships between the government and the peasants are very different now. He notes that the civil service is called the *pamong pradja*, and *pamong* means 'to look after the people who are not capable of looking after themselves'. And as in the ancient past, people who accumulate wealth are looked down upon, and every effort is made to separate them from their surplus. 'The state continues to feel,' Penny adds, 'that it is the only agency in society that has the right or ability to tell the common people what to do; and the people who have government jobs feel that it is they alone, by virtue of their position, who should live well – and high military and civil officials do live well for the most part.' In their belief that economic activities should be guided and controlled, government officials have also built up a mammoth

1. ibid., p. 20.

of complex regulations which tend to hinder, rather than encourage and stimulate economic growth. Further, Penny argues, such is the paternalism of officialdom, feeling it should 'do everything for the common people', little is left to the initiative of the farmer.

I have travelled extensively throughout the Indonesian archipelago, and my observations generally support these views. However, I will confine my remarks mainly to Central Java. Few regions, I believe, are likely to become more sensitive barometers of the success or shortcomings of the Suharto administration's economic efforts. Central Java is a region that has remained a source of concern for the government. The residue of support Sukarno retained among its people was a major cause of Suharto's cautious and somewhat inconclusive handling of his predecessor's overthrow, and the inroads the Communist Party (PKI) and the Nationalist Party (PNI) made among the region's civilian and military administrative apparatus still seriously handicap central government control. Moreover, the legacy of hate and fear arising from the post-*coup* killings, the general apathy and suspicion found among the people towards central authority and the increasing military presence, and the religious and political turmoil caused by the change in government, have all helped complicate the general situation. But the heart of the problem lies in the poverty and backwardness of the province's grossly excessive and potentially politically explosive population.

Central Java is certainly no Kosala. The beauty is often there – the lofty volcanic peaks, their cones often wreathed in cloud, the rolling hills and the emerald plains. But unlike the fabled kingdom of the Ramayana legend, there is far from a surfeit of fertile soil, while periodic famine and flooding are common-place occurrences. From the air, clusters of trees mark out the villages fighting for space amid the yellow-green paddy fields that often stretch high up the lava-flecked slopes of still active volcanoes, and among the white chalk of porous, infertile limestone outcrops. About twenty-five million people live within this

21

region of less than 15,000 square miles (two per cent of Indonesia's land mass, and about one-sixth the size of the Australian state of Victoria). Its farming lands are the most crowded in the world, reaching more than one million people on about 1,600 acres in the district of Klaten (between the ancient cities of Solo and Jogjakarta) where the village of Wedi lies. The people are also among the poorest, growing mainly rice, maize and cassava for their own needs, and rubber, sugar, coffee, tea, cocoa and other crops for sale. There are a few more exotic exports from among the coastal fishermen – sharks fins to Hong Kong, shrimps to the Netherlands, and seaweed to Japan – but total income from exports rarely amounts to much. A little oil has been found, and there are manganese mines near Jogjakarta, but generally the province is best known abroad as the home of the magnificent Borobudur monument and the Prambanan temple complex.

Whereas the ancient agrarian empires had plenty of land for expansion, today in Central Java, about two-thirds of the province is already under intensive cultivation and further lands are no longer available for new development. With a population that has nearly doubled in the past forty years, the pressure for land and employment has reached staggering proportions. Apart from the landless, latest estimates show that less than three farmers in a thousand own more than about twelve acres; four-fifths have less than three acres; more than half, barely one acre; and one-third, about half-an-acre. The problems that this population growth creates as it continues to add more than 600,000 new mouths each year are enormous. In the field of education alone, the fact that more than forty per cent of the population is below the age of fourteen means that probably less than a third can get even a few years' elementary schooling with existing facilities. Likewise, health facilities are completely inadequate with the government providing less than 10,000 hospital beds for the entire province.

One consequence of the pressure for land is to make the

already conservative, superstitious peasant farmers even more subsistence minded. Concerned foremost with security, which they equate with land and low-value subsistence crops like rice rather than produce for fluctuating commercial markets, they may often ignore the most profitable opportunities available to them. (Some observers, however, dispute this point, see p. 33). Willy-nilly, they are also forced into the excessive use of labour. Rice is still harvested head by head with a hand-held knife of the kind that was discarded in Europe many centuries ago. Angry neighbours are known to have burned one farmer's rice crops when he began using a sickle simply because this technological innovation threatened the livelihood of many landless and unemployed. As a result, nowhere else in the world is so much labour employed for so little economic result. And not only do most farmers fail to protect their plants and animals from pests and diseases, some may even refuse when urged to do so because this might make 'the gods angry' and cause them to send plague and famine upon the people.

During 1968, in an effort to change this situation, the Central Java provincial administration launched a programme of rural development which it calls 'village modernization'. Noting that twelve of the province's twenty-nine districts were already suffering annual food shortages, the Central Java Governor, Major General Munadi, commented on the 'ever growing number of unemployed and beggars in the cities', the 'disguised unemployment', and the 'challenge to educators that schools should not produce unemployable people'. Farmers, he said, were often caught in a cycle of chronic debt. Forced to sell their crops, often at deflated prices fixed while they were still green in the field, to those who had lent them money, their land also was becoming the property of money-lenders. The remedy, Munadi asserted, lay partly in a change of 'mental attitude'. 'The main aim is to change our mental attitude from looking upon the rural areas as an "object" of our political, social, economic and cultural activities, into an attitude in which the rural area becomes a "subject" which plays an active role in making our political, and especially our socio-economic decisions.' Specifically, Munadi argued, rural areas 'must free themselves from the control of individuals, brokers and money lenders who hold crops as security . . . and decide prices themselves'.

During mid-1969, I visited Central Java to try to find out what 'village modernization' meant. It was my sixth visit to the region over a period of nearly three years, and during earlier visits I had met the governor and a wide range of military, civilian and political leaders in the region, as well as people from all walks of life. I had also seen village conditions in various parts of the province. I especially recall my first contact with the governor's office in Semarang in 1967. During a meeting with Munadi, who had not long been provincial governor, he had called in some of his staff to answer questions put by myself and a colleague, Stanley Karnow, of the *Washington Post*. His staff were permanent civil servants, inherited from the previous governor, and I remember leaving the meeting staggered at the 'Alice in Wonderland' twist to so many of their replies to the questions we had asked. If they had any real grasp of the problems they confronted, this was well concealed. It was almost as if they were living in another world, hermetically sealed off from the villages about them. With this recollection, I returned to the governor's office in mid-1969.

I was ushered into the 'Operation's room' for a briefing on the overall situation. 'Operation's rooms' are now a 'must' for all provincial administrative centres. They were introduced by Suharto for keeping a close check on the national economic and development drive, and especially to help with the successful implementation of the Five-Year Development Plan. Generally, they follow the pattern of a quite successful system developed in neighbouring Malaysia, but whereas all regional 'Operation's rooms' in Malaysia follow a standard format, those in

Indonesia vary from region to region. In fact, some were hastily thrown together on the eve of a presidential visit mainly to comply with central government orders, and include alleged 'facts' that officials privately admit are largely imaginative. A number, with their elaborate charts and diagrams, also give greater evidence of undoubted artistic skills than an understanding of economics. In Semarang, a large room is given over to maps, charts and other paraphernalia of planning. During reporting sessions, officials sit at map-covered tables and speak into tape recorders so that they can later be reminded of their comments if their individual targets and predictions are not met. A series of huge charts showing progress in red (overdue), black (on schedule) and green (ahead of schedule) slide in and out of view at the flick of a switch at one end of the room, giving what is meant to be an up-to-the-minute run-down on the province's economic and social development projects, but a cursory glance showed that some reports had not even been entered.

The secretary of the 'Operation's room' was a pleasant, slightly built Javanese civil servant, dressed in jungle green. He explained the general layout, and then asked if I had any questions. I began by asking what changes were sought in 'modernizing' the village. He ignored this, and launched into an obvious spiel. 'Our basic aim is to raise the living standards of people – to increase their per capita income,' he said. I interrupted for an estimate of their present 'per capita income'. He could not say, but the public relations officer suggested a figure ranging from $50 to $80, then later asked that this be reported as 'less than $80 a year'. The 'Op's room' secretary continued: 'The aim of the Five-Year Development Plan is to raise per capita income, and this can only be achieved by increasing production. How? Well we have land and water, manpower, skills and capital. The real problem is with the latter two – skills and capital. We are lacking these.' (He did not mention another 'resource' listed on a wall chart – the 'spiritual' resource. Perhaps, he believed a foreigner could not be expected to comprehend such a notion, or perhaps, he himself was not especially convinced of its relevance.) 'In order to raise production', he continued, 'and to make use of available resources, we need more modern infrastructure, such as communications. Why? In order to market produce . . .'

As he was losing momentum, I asked what was meant by 'modernization'. He explained that agricultural facilities should be 'modernized' since the first aim was to increase agricultural production. He gave as examples the use of water pumps and 'modern techniques of cultivation', mentioning tractors in this context. He then referred to new rice growing techniques, the establishment of rice mills, and the possible installation of silos for storing rice. As I continued to probe the idea of 'modernization', I was told that 'in the past the village had been made an "object" of the middleman', but now the 'aim is to make the village a "subject".' 'The government is trying to change the mental attitude of villagers, and especially of the village leaders. For example, in the past, many villagers lacked understanding in the use of fertilizers – how much to apply, and which were the best. The old yields averaged about 30 quintals (about 3 tons) a hectare (2½ acres). With new techniques, yields are now averaging 40 and may reach 50 quintals per hectare.' [He did not mention what I later learned – that for the farmer the increased production meant much lower prices. Whereas before five kilos (1 kilo = 2.2 lbs.) of rice might buy material for new clothes, now he needed ten kilos. And not all that unreasonably, the farmer was asking why he should produce more rice only to find himself worse off than before.]

Turning from village 'modernization', I began asking questions about rice production. Unable to answer, he called for the appropriate argicultural expert, whom I asked for an estimate of Central Java's rice needs. The expert could not say, but quickly reeled off the target the province was *aiming* for. This was easily derived from the targeted national consumption per person dreamed up on the planning boards in Jakarta. The other, he would have had to work out for himself, but he did not seem to have reliable figures on how much rice was being produced in Central Java, and how much was being imported or exported. And as all kinds of sly dealings revolve around the farmers' main food crop, and the country's staple diet, this perhaps was not especially surprising. But the simple fact is that countless officials throughout Indonesia are today attempting to reach production 'targets' without knowing where they start from, or without having any real way of knowing when they have achieved them. Even so, if figures are needed for official reports, they will be found, regardless of whether or not they have any real basis in fact.

I mention this episode to underline an obvious point which is sometimes lost sight of by visiting foreign officials who talk only with the top, highly knowledgeable and articulate echelon of the Indonesian administration. The success or failure of the present government's efforts to improve the lot of the peasant will ultimately be decided not in the conference rooms in Jakarta, but at village level in the field. No matter how able and dedicated its economic advisers and planners – as is presently the case – the administration's best made plans can quickly come apart in the regions through lack of interest and understanding among second and third level officials. This is appreciated in Jakarta, and in Central Java by Munadi himself, who was aware that not all his staff understood what he was trying to do. Partly the problem lies in the educational background of many of these officials. They are often trained in politics and administrative law rather than agricultural extension and sociology. But the problem goes much deeper, since it also involves the yawning gap that generally exists between officialdom and the village people, which even men like Munadi and officials in Jakarta often seem to ignore.

It is the problem of the 'we' and the 'they'. 'We' are the better educated – the urban élite. 'They' are the 'people' – the *rakjat*, as they are often patronizingly called. 'We' are

27

the leaders, the thinkers, the people on whom the 'they'
depend. Overtones of this attitude are found among most
groups in the urban societies – among the military, the
civilian bureaucracy, the students and so on. It is true that
many of the 'we' were originally born in the villages – and
this they will often stress. But they gladly leave that world
behind when they join the urban élite, though again many
will stress how they love to return to their villages – for a
short visit! There are two broad aspects of the new status
ex-villagers may acquire in their new surroundings – education and office. Especially among the Javanese, an educated person acquires what is sometimes called a 'teacher
complex'. With a little learning, he becomes aloof from
his more humble origins. 'They' – the people – must now
come to him. It is part of the Javanese way of life. And this
'teacher' henceforth will hold court dispensing his 'knowledge' – which rarely will have much bearing on the practical side of life. The status accorded office is equally
important. Irrespective of the man's ability, it is the position he holds that really counts in the eyes of the people.
And it is a deeply ingrained attitude which few Indonesians appear to do anything to discourage.

One consequence of the problem of the 'we' and the
'they' is a seemingly unbridgeable communication gap.
Officials, be they civilian or military, can no longer talk
'with' rather than 'to' villagers on a person-to-person basis.
It is a situation that is felt by official and villager alike
since both are a party to this traditional relationship. At
the same time, it is a relationship that is accepted fatalistic-
ally by many villagers and with a good deal of apathy and
suspicion. They have learned that it pays to be deferent to
authority, but this does not mean they co-operate willingly
with authority's requests. The Javanese have seven ways of
saying 'yes', and depending on how it is pronounced, the
same word can mean anything from 'yes' to 'maybe' or
even an insulting 'no'. It's always a great source of amuse-
ment for village people when a puppeteer plays upon this
word during a shadow theatre performance, having a ser-

vant of the king reply to commands in the different tones. The audience is delighted by the way the servant insults his master and ruler while the latter is supposedly unaware of the intended insult.

For as long as the villager can remember, 'authority' has always been telling him to produce more. Whether it was his ancient forefathers under the rulers of the Mataram or Madjapahit, or more recently under Dutch colonial rule, or since independence, he has always been exhorted to work harder and grow more. And his experience – and that of his people before him – has been that usually, though not always, whatever he produces over and above his minimal needs will be taken from him in some way or another. In this frame of mind, he automatically tends to greet each new request (or promise) with increasing scepticism and suspicion, though his polite smile may continually grow broader.

It is also comparatively easy for the city dweller to take advantage of his country cousin, since, living amid endemic underemployment, the latter has no idea of the real worth of his labour. For instance, in a village, the owner of a house has no comprehension of its possible worth in an urban setting. He has not paid much for the labour. His neighbours helped build it at little or no charge, and he, perhaps, provided some food for a party when the building was finished. As a result, urban traders will buy up teak houses in the village at bargain prices, move them to the town, and sell them for exorbitant profits. Likewise, the average farmer often has no real inkling of what his farm produce brings on the world market. And even if he did, he has no effective platform on which he can express his point of view. The politicians in the towns and cities who profess to have his interests at heart more often than not belong to the 'we' than the 'they'.

Officialdom partly recognizes the communication gap by seeking the services of puppeteers to spread its propaganda through the shadow plays. In fact, anyone with a message to get across to the 'people' tries to capitalize on the often extraordinary talents of these professional performers. Something of an anachronism in his social setting, the puppeteer remains a part of two worlds. On the one hand, he must be well-read in traditional literature and folklore, have an excellent general knowledge of contemporary affairs, a high degree of musical skill, a retentive memory, be a fine orator and a capable mimic, and possess immense physical stamina to survive the night-long non-stop performances. At the same time, he must remain a 'man of the people', since only by living close to the people can he acquire the necessary intimate knowledge of each region's special idiosyncrasies, and so fully win his audience's confidence and genuine affection. Of course, for the would-be propagandists this presents problems, since ultimately the puppeteers' loyalty rests with the 'they', and many are even more adept at 'making fun of' the 'we' than promoting their cause.

For the villager, the shadow theatre is both a form of escape from his humdrum daily existence and a primary means by which his fatalistic acceptance of his 'lot' in life is generally reinforced and perpetuated. Its stories usually reaffirm the helplessness of the ordinary mortal in determining his own fate, depicting him largely as a pawn in a vast game played by mysterious cosmic forces. It also inculcates values and attitudes among the people that bar social change, such as the folly of tampering with timeless traditions or questioning the wisdom of one's elders. At the same time, the shadow theatre is also the repository of a way of life that contains much that is truly admirable. It is also a magnificent ancient art which one can only hope will never die.

In Central Java, I was told, there are at least 4,000 puppeteers – amateur and professional – performing among the provinces' 8,400-odd villages and towns. Not all have won the acclaim of Ki Raden Sunartosabdho, who despite his titles, still wins acceptance as a 'man of the people'. Born in the village of Wedi in 1925, the youngest of a family of eight children, Sunartosabdho is a remarkable man – self-educated, engaging, and delighted to talk with me about his calling even though I had unwittingly disturbed him in the mid-morning following an all night performance. A self-confessed shadow theatre fanatic since the age of twelve, he admits his fame really spread following a performance broadcast over the national radio network in 1957. A big, heavily built man, with thick black hair, kindly, intelligent eyes and a friendly pock-marked face, he can now command as much as $500 a performance – a princely sum far beyond the resources of village people, but not of the 'we' within the cities requiring the puppeteers' services. And like most puppeteers, he obligingly plays for very flexible fees!

Early 1969, as the Five-Year Development Plan was launched, Sunartosabdho was summoned to Jakarta for a 'command performance' at the palace. He later returned to Central Java, well rewarded for his skills, and with a special message from the President. 'Please do your task and duty well as a puppeteer,' he said he was told. 'And in performing a puppet show, you should include the real meaning of the Five-Year Plan so that people will know this and give the plan their full support.' In Semarang, he received a similar 'message' from Governor Munadi, who asked especially that he should explain the question of 'rural modernization'. Sunartosabdho is happy to oblige, and does not think the shadow theatre will suffer too much if used for educational ends, though he admits this will depend on how the puppeteer goes about the task. He played excerpts from some taped performances which advised villagers to educate themselves through the 'do-schools' – an idea Munadi has borrowed from the United States for trying to impart technical skills to rural peoples. 'I hope that the "do-schools" will also include a school for puppeteers,' Sunartosabdho jokingly tells his audience. Then he urges them towards 'auto-activity' – 'activating' themselves so that they may become more prosperous, and so that their prosperity might spill out into the towns as well. They are told that the towns have already 'modernized' themselves, so that it was up to the villagers to follow suit. But they must also 'elevate' themselves from the status of an 'object' to that of a 'subject', deciding their own 'destiny and future'. On this note, the performance broke into the province's special song honouring 'rural modernization'.

Sunartosabdho is just one of scores of puppeteers pressed into service in Central Java to spread the gospel of village 'modernization' and the virtues of the Five-Year Development Plan. Among Indonesians, reactions as to the likely impact of the puppeteers upon the people are hesitant and varied. But most quickly mention that this has all been tried before by Sukarno under Guided Democracy, and that those efforts petered out after a few years without producing notable change. And often in even stronger terms, some knowledgeable Javanese privately express doubts about Munadi's efforts at 'village' or 'rural modernization'. These people assert that although he talked about changing 'mental attitudes', his programme was still largely being imposed upon the village people from above. Likewise, they may show you a pamphlet or two dealing with the setting up of village co-operatives, and the right way to go about working among village people. These, you find, tell officials and leaders: 'In the foreground you set an example; in the middle ground you develop a will to work among the people; and in the background you apply pressure to get things working.' It is written by a Javanese who certainly does not lack an understanding of the situation, they explain, but the problem is finding officials who are prepared to put it into practice. [Though you learn from the senior army intelligence officer in the province that cadres of the now outlawed Communist Party clandestinely still practise what they call the 'three togethers' – work together (with the villager), eat together, and sleep together.] Similarly, the same sources comment that if Munadi's 'do-schools' are to succeed, the teachers must also 'do'. Early experience in attempting to give teachers a more practical frame of mind apparently produced a reaction of revolt at the idea of getting their hands 'soiled' with the grit and grime of the practical side of life. But all agree that more practical teaching is vital.

Travelling through the province in 1969, I also found a great deal of confusion and disagreement over the question of *whose* 'mental attitudes' really needed changing. For instance, few deny that the villagers have long been the 'object' of rapacious outside interests, but whereas Munadi may suggest the main villain is the money-lender who shackles the farmer with usurious interest rates, an Indonesian economist (also a Javanese) puts another point of view. 'What does the government do?' he asks. 'It builds an impressive bank in Jogjakarta or some other major town. It is open only in the morning, so if a farmer can overcome his normal reluctance to approach an aloof official in his grand city setting, he must take the morning off from work to do so, and travel from his village. On the other hand, even though his interest rates are higher, the money-lender does travel to the village, and is available at the villager's convenience. What the government should provide are on-the-spot banks, open in the evenings when farmers have finished their work in the fields.' (More recently, the Suharto administration has begun developing services of this kind through the use of mobile banking units. However, some observers doubt whether cheaper credit will help until the farmers begin to feel more economically secure, since they still tend to use credit for consumption rather than investment.) The same Indonesian economist, who has been conducting surveys among village people, also believes that the lack of economic 'know-how' often lies less with the farmer than the educated Javanese officials or administrators who profess to be putting him on the path to prosperity. 'Too many officials still regard themselves as above the "dirty" business of commerce. The farmer often knows which crops will give the best returns. His main problem is with government policies which keep upsetting his calculations. For instance, he may be obliged to grow rice for government purchase at unrealistically low prices when he knows another crop would be more profitable.'

Others with whom I talked were more concerned about the inroads the military were making into Central Java. 'During the period immediately following the *coup*,' one eminent Javanese civilian asserted, 'the army gave us security. From October 1965 until March 1966 while the Communist Party was still strong, it often was not safe to sleep in one's own house. But the army restored security, and this gave them a bank balance. Since then, they have been drawing on this credit, and many people are beginning to think they are already overdrawn.' Voicing a widely held feeling, he added: 'The trouble is the army is a political party. And it is behaving just like the political parties in the past. Too many are simply in the business of earning a living. They won't work with their hands because that is beneath their dignity. So when they go into the village, it is either to give orders or to engage in some form of extortion. And they ride roughshod over everything, never consulting anyone. The real problem is – who will discipline the disciplinarians?'

If these comments and observations seem on the excessively gloomy side, a brief summary of one aspect of the problem may prove useful. During the present decade, Indonesia's population will climb to more than 150 million people. Something like twenty million people born since the early fifties will be flooding on to an already saturated labour market. And roughly half of the new mouths needing food, and the new hands wanting work, will be found among the already overcrowded farming lands of Central and East Java. Even if the government was doing anything significant about family planning and population control – which it is not – this could only have a very marginal effect on the population explosion in the region in the next decade or so. Likewise, even if the government were able to carry out a massive resettlement programme – which it cannot – this also would hardly have any real impact on the overall problem.

While the so-called 'green revolution' – brought about by new high-yield strains of rice – does offer some hope, Indonesia has not got off to a very good start in this regard. Despite extensive plantings of the new varieties, rice production rose only marginally during 1969, and imports of about 800,000 tons were twenty-five per cent higher than the previous year. Poor weather was largely to blame, but the administration of the government sponsored programme for boosting rice production became the cause of a national scandal during 1970, forcing Suharto to curtail its activities. Called BIMAS, the programme was conducted in co-operation with both private Indonesian and foreign firms, which provided fertilizers, pesticides and other services on credit under a government guarantee, in an attempt to force the pace of development. Corruption, political obstruction and plain bad management largely brought about the scheme's failure, costing the government, according to some press reports, about $20 million, and casting grave doubts on the likelihood of the administration reaching its targeted increase of nearly forty-seven per cent in rice production during the period of the Five-Year Development Plan. During 1970, there were also signs of rising political agitation against the pressure targets imposed on the people responsible for implementing the Plan. In May, the vice-chairman of the parliamentary commission dealing with agriculture, Rachmat Rangkuti, expressed the hope that future projects for intensifying agricultural production should not stress targets but concentrate on 'improving the lot of the farmers, not as pawns in the game, as has so far been the case, but as masters of their own fate'. He asserted the government's BIMAS project had been far too ambitious.

Even so, the picture is not one of unrelieved gloom. The BIMAS project was far from a complete failure. In some regions, it did demonstrate what could be done. With better methods, crop yields can be considerably raised on existing agricultural lands. Some agriculturalists believe increases of two to even four times present levels are possible with most crops, and further scientific discoveries that could increase existing potential are also possible. However, if these potentials are ever to be realized, much will depend on the incentives and the sense of economic security the government can provide for farmers. Suharto has shown concern over this aspect of the problem, including the need for farmers to receive a fairer return for their produce and be able to buy fertilizers and pesticides at reasonable prices. But he will have to get much tougher with his civilian and military administrators if he is to translate his concern into tangible results.

There are hopeful signs too in smaller things. Not everyone is waiting for the government to solve all the economic problems. In Central Java, for instance, one headmaster solved the question of unpaid school fees by having the students turn part of the sports field into a vegetable garden. Within two years, they were not only selling enough produce to pay their own fees, but were also getting a practical education in gardening and simple marketing. In another instance, a community of religious nuns running an orphanage successfully turned to raising poultry to solve both their financial and nutritional problems. Some socially aware teachers are also sending the children of more affluent parents out among the poor to make simple surveys of how these people manage to survive. Invariably, the children are amazed by what they learn. And while these kinds of things may sound elementary and insignificant in comparison with the enormity of the problem, some Indonesians believe they are the first basic steps towards its solution. In the view of these people, the national dream of an Indonesian 'Kosala' will never come alive through planning and endless conferences in Jakarta, but only through a growing awareness among scores of thousands of more privileged Indonesians that the solution lies in their own practical efforts.

Chapter 2

The Search For Unity

I do not vouch for every detail in the three sketches that follow. But the people are real, and, I believe, the essential points about them are accurate. Their stories are recounted here for reasons I will explain.

*

In a cave high among the mountains of West Java, Girang Adjal was meditating. He had eaten no food for two days, and only occasionally had drunk from a vessel containing palm wine, or from a spring surging miraculously from within the cave. At times he had dozed fitfully, but he continually fought the desire to sleep. Now his whole body felt light and free, almost as if he might float away. His tiredness had vanished, and his senses seemed especially acute.

Through the gloom of the cave, Girang Adjal was aware of his two colleagues, chieftains Kais and Ajah, motionless in their meditation. He felt a warm glow of pride as he thought of their three villages clustered in a protective ring about the source of the 'waters of 'life'. This cave – the sacred *Domas* – and the waters that surged from the spring it sheltered were the source of no ordinary river, no matter what others might think. What of the scores of thousands who depended on its life-giving waters? In their ignorance they knew of it only as the Tji Udjung – just another river, gathering momentum as it tumbled down the foothills to sweep through the town of Rangkasbitung, and across the alluvial plains of Bantam. These people drank its waters, washed in them, cooked with them; they tapped them for irrigating their paddy fields; and they dumped their refuse in them. By the time the Tji Udjung spilled out into the Java Sea some forty-five miles west of Jakarta, it was a thick muddy brown giant sewer of the dead, rotten and decaying. Only at its source, high among the hills in the shadow of Mount Malang, did the waters of Tji Udjung remain pure and undefiled.

In the stillness of the breaking dawn, Girang Adjal wondered at the enormity of the task the *Batara tunggal* — the 'One Supreme God' — had set for his people in choosing them to guard the purity of life as symbolized in the source of the Tji Udjung. He marvelled at the wisdom of his ancestors in realizing that only by retreating from the profanities and pollution of man-made 'progress' could they hope to succeed. The hardship and sacrifice involved paled into insignificance compared with the loftiness and importance of their mission. For should they succeed, the *Batara tunggal* would one day return to rule over a just and prosperous world — of that he was certain.

He remembered times when he had entertained doubts about the wisdom of his people's ways. The poverty, the harshness of their life, and especially the inflexibility of their *adat* — the timeless customs and traditions by which they all lived — had caused him to waver. But then he hadn't really understood, as he did now, as a guardian of his people's rich heritage. *Adat* was truly all-embracing. It determined so many things — ceremonies of birth, marriage and death, when and how to plant and harvest crops, pray for rain, or build houses . . . Yes, *adat* was the well-spring of his authority among his people — the power of the past working in the present for an unchanging future. Amid the many uncertainties of life, *adat* was something to hold on to, a life-raft by which to remain afloat, a sheet-anchor against doubt and despair, and a cause for endless comfort. He would guard it with his last breath.

There was little doubt Islam would have destroyed their *adat*, Girang Adjal reflected. Even now, the danger had not passed. The roads . . . the outside world . . . continued to draw closer, although his own village, Tjibeo, was still a two-day trek through jungle from the nearest road. But some of his people had fled their harsh life, even embracing Islam. Others, while unable to live under their strict code, also could not snap the umbilical cord that tied them to their ancient past. They now lived under easier laws on the outskirts of their lands. They no longer worried about leaving the jungle, or travelling by bus and train, or using money circulated by the outside world. They talked with strangers. Some even read the Koran. At times, he wondered how much longer his people could hope to keep their way of life.

Girang Adjal wondered too about the mystery of life. What was a society that did not recognize the divine power of the *sakti* – that strange, mysterious life-force animating all things and controlling the movement of the entire universe? It was in the air he breathed, the rock on which he now squatted, the waters flowing lustily before him. It pervaded the mountains in which he and his people lived, the earth they tilled, the jungles they scoured for fruits and honey. It enveloped the entire universe. How could people understand the nature of things when they cut down the jungles and drove the spirits into seeking refuge among the mountains, the volcanic craters, and even the ocean beds? Only he and his people who lived among the spirits could 'feel' – and therefore 'know' – the nature of things. He often realized this as he sat by his house in the cool evenings watching the night creeping in through the jungles to drive out the day, or as the angry spirits whipped up the swirling black clouds to engulf the mountains about them. What was 'progress' and 'change' when it destroyed the harmony of nature, and upset the spirits of our ancestors?

The full light of the morning sun suddenly flooded the *Domas*. The vigil was over. Chieftain Girang Adjal rose to his feet, his dark, honey-coloured skin glistening in the sun. He flashed a smile of greeting as his two colleagues stirred. He knew what prophecy and guidance they must give their people in these troubled times. President Sukarno would fall. That was the revelation he, Adjal, had received during their two-day fast and meditation in the sacred cave. The great, proud man had abused his power, which must now pass to other hands. The leaders in Jakarta would be told. He would send an emissary right away. He thought of the long journey which must be made on foot and suddenly felt tired. His whole body ached. All the exhilaration was gone.

*

Daud Beureueh gazed out through the tangle of foliage that pressed in upon the medley of timber, iron, bamboo and thatched palm leaves that was his house. He could see a flat sweep of paddy land for which Pidié was famed. Pidié surely was the rice-bowl of Atjeh and the backbone of the province's struggling economy; a broad expanse of fertile alluvial plain ringed by mountains and running down to the seas of the Malacca Straits -- that busy ocean highway so intimately linked with Atjeh's past fortunes.

Daud thought of his village: a scattered collection of huts eight miles inland from the town of Sigli. Here he had no telephone, no piped house-water, no city-style sanitation. It was not like the big house that might have been his in Jakarta had he so wished. But this was home. Here he had been born, had lived, and, he hoped, would die. This was the village he had made famous, and whose name he now so proudly bore. Daud of Beureueh ... Who in Atjeh had not heard of him? Here he was 'Father' among his people -- the man others knelt before to kiss his hand. Who in Jakarta won that kind of respect?

It was strange, he thought, in many ways he had left his village as a teenage child only to return something of a stranger among his own people. How long ago? He scarcely could remember, his body frail now, wasted by time and the ravages of dank, mosquito-ridden jungle retreats. When was he born? ... 1317 ... or 1897 by the calendar of the Western world. He thought automatically in the Muhammadan year, for he, Daud, the 'Lion of Atjeh', lived by the commands of Allah, and Muhammad was his prophet.

Aged fifteen, he recalled, he had left for the school for advanced Islamic studies at Eulebeu. It was not far from the village of Beureueh. Yet, somehow, it was a world away. For nine years he had remained, and he had emerged a new man. He was born again with a vision of man and the 'law' transcending the confining views of *adat* and traditional village life. With his new knowledge he recalled, he could hardly help but pity his own people for their ignorant, shallow lives. He knew that the communal bonds that once tied him to his village had been snapped for all time. A new rope now bound him to a much wider world – a rope that did not rot in the rain, nor crack in the sun. And it was a rope that freed, even as it bound; the rope of Allah, the one true God.

How often had he explained to his people that in the beginning God created the angels out of light? The earth and the natural world, He made from nothingness. From the earth came Adam, and from Adam's rib, Hawa, the first woman. To Adam – and so to all men – God gave both an animal-like nature, passion, and also the ability to know, reason. His passion leads man away from God: away from salvation. But reason allows him to control his instincts, learn to know God's will, and ultimately regain the paradise lost through eating the forbidden fruit. Reason too leads man to a sensibly governed, peaceful and prosperous world.

History, like the turning wheel, reflected the waxing and waning of 'reason' and 'passion' among men. Take Atjeh for instance. Six centuries ago the first Muslim states of Southeast Asia had emerged here. Under the unifying power of 'reason', the mighty sultanate of Atjeh arose three centuries later, becoming during the early decades of the seventeenth century under Sultan Iskandar Muda a powerful political centre, and the gateway to Mecca in the East. What Atjehnese does not swell with pride recalling those glorious days when the city of Banda Atjeh was among the great cities of the world? Indians, Arabs, Turks, Chinese, Persians, Abysinnians . . . peoples from all points of the globe flocked to its doors. A truly cosmopolitan place, wisely ruled under Islamic laws, Atjeh was at its zenith, and Islam was truly alive. But then came the dark days. Passions overcame reason. Quarrels arose. Region was set against region. The rope of unity grew slack, and Atjeh slept. Now, Atjeh was awakening again; a new era had dawned.

Hadn't he, Daud Beureueh, played an important part in this re-awakening? Among all the Islamic leaders of Atjeh, wasn't he most often compared with the great Habid – the famed reformist leader of the last century, who had moved fearlessly throughout the countryside boldly condemning the evils of cock-fighting, gambling, opium smoking and illicit intercourse? How often had he, Daud, trod the same paths as Habid and the other great scholars Atjeh had known?

Daud Beureueh recalled also the struggle against the Dutch; their defeat by the Japanese; and then the crushing of the Uleebelang. He could not help but feel contempt for the Uleebelang – Atjehnese chieftains under the Sultans of former times and the aristocrats of the past. They had bled the people of profits from their pepper gardens, lorded it over all, and flouted Allah's laws. Cock-fighting, gambling, opium smoking and illicit intercourse were all infamous Uleebelang vices. When the Sultanate fell, the Uleebelang had sold out to the Dutch. When the Japanese were defeated, the Uleebelang tried to seize power in Atjeh. And Jakarta had turned a deaf ear to his appeals for help. But in a short, bloody struggle, his followers had routed the Uleebelang. In Pidié, he proudly recalled, not a single Uleebelang escaped with his life.

Then came the betrayal. Above all, he blamed Sukarno. How vividly he still remembered the half-starved, tattered band of men Sukarno sent seeking aid from Atjeh during the armed struggle against the Dutch following the proclamation of independence. Atjeh had given them two kilos of gold to buy the first two planes the Republic owned. And how many thousands of refugees from Medan and other parts of Sumatra had Atjeh fed and clothed during those trying times? Repeatedly Sukarno had promised that the Indonesian state would be based on Islamic law, and if that were not possible, at least it would be so in Atjeh. He still remembered Sukarno, weeping, imploring him for help. But far from keeping his promises, Sukarno wanted only to crush Atjeh. Was it any wonder that he, Daud, had led his people in revolt?

In 1953, he had withdrawn into the mountains and jungles and for eight long years held out against the might of Jakarta. Gradually, he had won his points. In 1956, Atjeh again became a province, and later, gained full autonomy in religious affairs. Finally, late in 1968, the provincial legislature in Banda Atjeh enacted Islamic law within the province. Jakarta demurred, but what could the central government do? These, laws are what the Atjehnese people want.

And the state philosophy of *Pantja Sila*? What does it mean? Belief in One God, in Nationality, in Humanity, in Democracy, and in Social Justice . . . It is the creation of Sukarno, and tailored to Javanese tastes. Well Sukarno has fallen from power, but Jakarta still clings stubbornly to the shibboleth of *Pantja Sila* that has never been properly examined, and never really discussed. He recalled telling General Suharto as much in a meeting in Jakarta some time ago. Everyone interprets *Pantja Sila* in his own way. How can Indonesia ever be strongly united by such vague beliefs? Real unity was only possible under the rope of God; through a state ruled by Islamic law. Then again reason would prevail. Well, Atjeh will lead the way.

*

The roar of the twin outboards sent a flock of parakeets screeching aloft to become lost against an horizon of endless jungle. A crocodile, sunning on a sandbar, slipped silently into the water. The speed-boat swerved sharply, avoiding a partly submerged log. The bow waves surged in angry protest, then just as suddenly subsided. Ahead the waters looked cool, tranquil and inviting. For two days they had been winding up the Kapuas – the mighty inland waterway that arose in the heartland of Kalimantan (Borneo) among the slopes of the Muller ranges, then snaked through the jungles several hundred miles westward to spill into the South China sea. They had passed Sanggau and Sintang. Their destination – Putus Sibau – lay another day ahead. But slumped in the stern of the boat, Lai Pa Ka was lost in his own thoughts.

Lai Pa Ka knew his captors held two things especially against him – that he was a communist, and that he was Chinese. He suspected being Chinese was the more heinous offence in their eyes. Communists could change their views. But Chinese – could they ever be acceptable? That he doubted as he glanced about the boat. All were Indonesian soldiers from the army intelligence unit in Pontianak, West Kalimantan. In a way, he too was now one of them. He wore jungle fatigues like the others. But no pistol hugged his thigh; no carbine cradled in the crook of his arm. Was he a captive or turncoat? He had given himself up. Now he was working with the Indonesians attempting to persuade other Chinese guerrillas still hiding out in the jungles to surrender. But he knew he wasn't really trusted. And, he had to admit, not without cause.

How had he, Lai Pa Ka, switched sides? So much had happened, he thought, since the June night in 1963 when with a group of young Chinese he had slipped across the border from Sarawak into West Kalimantan. Nearly 1,000 Chinese from Sarawak had answered the Indonesian call for 'volunteers' for the 'Crush Malaysia' campaign. They had all changed their names to confuse the Sarawakian authorities. Overnight, Boon Kuet Fung had become Lai Pa Ka. But now the aliases meant nothing. Kuching and Pontianak were no longer at war but were working hand in glove. What an about-face in Indonesia since Sukarno had fallen from power and the fascist Suharto-Nasution clique had seized control!

Had it all begun for him at the Chung Hua Middle school in Kuching? Or was it enough to have been one of nine children born to a struggling Chinese trader? His friendship with Wong Kie Tjek, Huang Han and Yap Chung Hoo had begun in 1956 at the Chung Hua Middle school. He was seventeen, he recalled – an impressionable age. He had joined the clandestine Sarawak Advanced Youth Association at their instigation. Under their guidance, a new, hope-filled world had opened before him: a Sarawak freed from the oppression of British imperialism, the propertied classes, and the bourgeoisie. In this new Sarawak, workers and farmers would no longer be exploited, and all races – Dyaks, Chinese and Malay – would live peacefully under a progressive, revolutionary government guided by Marxism-Leninism and the wisdom of Mao Tse Tung.

But such a Sarawak could not come about without bloodshed. And not just in Sarawak and West Kalimantan – the whole region must inevitably become involved. Only through armed struggle could the 'new emerging forces' vanquish the 'old', and the 'have-nots' overcome the 'haves' . . . in Sarawak, all Kalimantan, and the whole of Southeast Asia. That was a dialectical truth; as certain as night follows day. That was why he, Lai Pa Ka, had answered the call when Sukarno had sought volunteers for the fight against the puppet Malaysian project. That was why his friend Yap Chung Hoo had already given his life in a brief, bloody armed clash with Indonesian forces in the Kalimantan jungles. And that was why Wong Kie Tjek continued to lead guerrilla forces among the remote mountain ranges north of Putus Sibau, towards which they were now speeding.

It was ironical, Lai Pa Ka thought, that Indonesia should have trained and equipped the forces that it now fought. Wong Kie Tjek commanded the North Kalimantan People's Army (PARAKU); Yap Chung Hoo, Huang Han, and he himself until his 'defection', had been among the key leaders of the Sarawak People's Guerrilla Movement (PGRS) During confrontation against Malaysia, both units had operated under Indonesian orders against

British and Malaysian security forces in forays across the border. Following the 1965 attempted *coup* in Jakarta, several attempts had been made to disarm and detain the units, but under orders from the 'Organization', they had simply melted into the jungle. Thus they sought to establish among the mountains of Kalimantan a 'liberated area' and 'revolutionary base', such as Mao Tse Tung had so successfully formed four decades ago among the mountains of Chingkangshan, and later in the caves of Yenan.

For two centuries, Lai Pa Ka reflected, Chinese had been settling in West Kalimantan. Mostly they were Hakkas and Teochius from Fukien and Kwangtung provinces. They had worked in the gold mines, developed agricultural lands, built boats, and involved themselves in local and export trade. Over the years, they had become by far the dominant economic force in the region. They now numbered more than 500,000; roughly a quarter of the population of West Kalimantan. For those Indonesians who saw all Chinese as a potential fifth-column, he knew this was alarming enough. But the geographical location of West Kalimantan, its proximity to other centres of Chinese power in Southeast Asia, and its comparatively easy access to Peking – all helped compound Indonesian uneasiness. And when the Chinese dominated PGRS and PARAKU began making their presence felt in Kalimantan, this uneasiness had turned to alarm.

But Lai Pa Ka believed the Indonesians were foolish if they thought they could solve this problem by herding the Chinese population into new settlements along the coasts. Already more than 50,000 had been forced to flee their shops and farms in the hinterland for the safety of the coastal towns of Pontianak, Mempawah and Singkawang following an outbreak of fighting with the Dyaks, and the failure of authorities to restore security in the region. Separating the Chinese from all they had worked for over the years only increased their bitterness and hate. It only intensified their awareness of being Chinese, binding them more closely to the 12 million-odd Chinese living throughout Southeast Asia, and forcing them to treasure their rich cultural heritage and links with Peking. The 'Organization' would be the long-term beneficiary of such policies as the authorities in West Kalimantan pursued.

Under interrogation, Lai Pa Ka had denied all knowledge of the 'Organization', except to admit he had read about its alleged existence in newspapers in Sarawak when Wong Kie Tjek was expelled by British authorities in 1961 for his communist activities. The 'Organization' was the close-knit communist leadership that had operated clandestinely for many years in Sarawak, extending its influence across the border into Kalimantan. It had gathered strength in the fifties, gradually acquiring a highly disciplined hard-core membership. Its influence was widespread among legally established political, social, economic and cultural bodies. But such was the level of secrecy surrounding its activities, even Lai Pa Ka did not know who the key leaders were. Certainly they were not Wong Kie Tjek and Huang Han, although both were highly placed, having trained in Peking. More recently also, he knew, the 'Organization' had joined forces with the remnants of the Indonesian Communist Party in West Kalimantan. In future, the two bodies would work closely together. Mao Tse Tung had spoken truly – Asians would indeed overrun Asians.

*

Nearly a century ago, novelist Joseph Conrad commented upon the 'brown, bronze, yellow faces, the black eyes, the glitter, the colour of an Eastern crowd . . . so old, so mysterious, resplendent and sombre'. Today, the same images unfold across the vast span of the Indonesian archipelago among the thousand-and-one faces of the complex human fabric inhabiting its islands . . . the dusky peasant tilling the picturesque paddy fields in Central and East Java, the grinning Makassarese crone peddling cigarettes from her roadside stall, the sharp-witted Minangkabau trader, the blunt-mannered, irrepressible Batak, the beautiful

47

Balinese dancer, the charmingly evasive Javanese official
. . . But they are much more than faces, as the stories of
Girang Adjal, Daud Beureueh and Lai Pa Ka make clear.
They are people with a widely varying sense of history,
incongruent values and attitudes to society, and a different
understanding about man, life and the need for change.
It follows too that such people will have very different
views about the kind of government the Republic should
establish, and the goals that government should pursue.
And none of this is especially surprising in view of the size,
location and legacies of the country and its people.

The Indonesian archipelago is the world's largest: a
sprawling network of more than 13,000 islands and islets
(of which about 3,000 are inhabited) flung across a giant
equatorial arc extending some 3,400 miles from east to
west, and 1,000 miles from north to south. Wedged between mainland Southeast Asia and continental Australia, the island complex is washed by two great seas –
the Indian and Pacific Oceans. Its location, its kaleido-
scopic landscapes of rugged ranges, lofty volcanic peaks,
rolling highlands, low-lying alluvial plains and tangled
jungles, and its vast inter-locking seas, have all wrought
a profound influence over the country's diverse history,
and contributed to the profusion of ethnic kind, language,
culture and social order found among its people.

The ancestors of most Indonesians probably first settled
parts of the archipelago 3,000 to 5,000 years ago. They were
Malays, thought originally to have come from southern
China. Some became farmers among the highly fertile
volcanic soils found inland on the islands of Java and Bali,
cultivating irrigated rice, and living in village settlements.
Others formed trading and fishing communities along the
coastal regions, and especially on the mouths of the larger
rivers of Java, Sumatra and Kalimantan (Borneo). Still
others led nomadic lives among the remoter, inland jungle
regions. But lying amid one of the world's oldest and
busiest waterways, the archipelago and its people could
scarcely remain isolated from the outside world. Well

before the birth of Christ, some of its inhabitants had established commercial links with China, trading pearls, precious stones, minerals, spices and timber. Other influences followed – Indian culture stimulated the rise of the noted kingdom-states of Srivijaya (South Sumatra), Mataram and Madjapahit (Java) from the seventh until the early sixteenth century; Islam gained a foothold late in the thirteenth century, spreading through the islands, especially in the fifteenth and sixteenth centuries; and the appearance of European empire and profit seekers in the region finally led to the establishment of Dutch colonial power in the archipelago early in the seventeenth century.

Out of this hotchpotch of history, after three-and-a-half years' war-time occupation by the Japanese, the Republic of Indonesia emerged through a unilateral declaration of independence by the indigenous people on 17 August 1945. And apart from the fact the Dutch wanted their former colony back after World War II, life proved far from tranquil for the fledgling state. Internal rebellion erupted even before the collapse of Dutch colonial power. Early in 1948, fanatical Muslim elements occupying jungle enclaves in West Java arbitrarily proclaimed an Islamic state (*Darul Islam*), beginning a fourteen year-long feud with the central government. Later in the same year, the radical 'left'tried to snatch power and impose communist rule on the Republic through a brief, abortive uprising centred in Madiun, East Java. Subsequently with the defeat of the Dutch late in 1949, opposition to government authority flared from time to time throughout the fifties in various parts of the archipelago, escalating into a major revolt in Sumatra and Sulawesi during 1957 and 1958 (commonly called the PRRI-Permesta rebellion).

Until the introduction of martial law in March 1957, the Republic was governed as a parliamentary democracy, with power mainly in the hands of political parties. With the failure of this form of government and the outbreak of regional rebellion, President Sukarno and the army emerged as the dominant forces, and together brought about the formal introduction of Guided Democracy in July 1959. But this system led to a protracted power struggle between Sukarno, the army and the Communist Party, which reached a climax in the October 1965 attempted *coup*.

From this brief glance at the origins and early turbulent years of the Republic, the tremendous challenge its diversity presents for establishing effective government and bringing about necessary social change and economic development becomes apparent. The figures of Girang Adjal, Daud Beureueh and Lai Pa Ka highlight the extremities of dissent and opposition to authority in post-independent Indonesia. As one of the leaders of the strange Baduis people, Girang Adjal represents only 2,000 to 3,000 people, and their 'protest' is silent, non-violent and largely ineffective. Daud Beureueh has a much wider influence among the Atjehnese people, but these account for barely two per cent of all Indonesians. Lai Pa Ka is not even native-born; an intruder on Indonesian soil. Even so, their highly disparate beliefs, values and attitudes towards man, society and the universe have far greater relevance within Indonesian society than their own immediate influence might suggest.

Girang Adjal and the Baduis people are not alone in clinging to an ancient past and animistic beliefs. Most Indonesians probably still believe that a 'soul' or 'life-force' (*sakti*) animates all things, and that the 'souls' of ancestors may continue to play an active role in their community life. Except in West Irian, cannibalism and head-hunting have given way to less violent ways of capturing the 'life-force' of another for the benefit of one's own person or community. But the Javanese who sucks (and swallows) the dying breath from the mouth of a distinguished figure is hoping to gain the magical power that accounted for that person's success in life. And many of the scores of millions who sit entranced by traditional Javanese shadow plays, may, in their hearts, be paying homage to their mythical ancestral heroes, whose wisdom and deeds they attempt to emulate in their everyday lives. In more recent times, many of these beliefs have suffered through increasing contact with more rational explanations of natural phenomena, but they still form an integral part of the way of life of countless people throughout the archipelago.

The vague, intuitive feeling that 'all life is one' through the medium of an invisible, divine energy – the flux of life flowing through gods, man, and all things, seen and unseen – is most powerfully fostered deep within the mountains where Girang Adjal and his people live, away from the harsh brutality of the noisy, man-made mechanical world. But city dwellers in large Indonesian towns have not lost their sense of respect for a real, all-pervasive spiritual world. Countless numbers have tales of magical and mystical experiences at their finger tips. And the delightful world of spirits the American scholar, Clifford Geertz, uncovered during his studies of Javanese life (some may be just practical jokers, others may give you a bad case of dysentery, while still others may prefer to sleep with your wife!) also find their enthusiastic following in the big cities and elsewhere throughout the archipelago. And while the Baduis are reputed to have few peers as experts in the occult arts – claiming clairvoyance, immunity from bullets and the powers of prophecy among their accomplishments – they by no means have a monopoly in these matters. Scores of mystical sects thrive, especially in Central and East Java. Soothsayers, mediums, spiritual advisers and holy men flourish in almost every village, and are patronized by the community leaders. Magically endowed objects such as stones, talismans, daggers, spears, masks, small shrines, and so on, are also the prized possessions of most people – from the President to the lowliest peasant.

As an indication of how seriously these matters are still regarded, take the case of Mbah Suro. Born in 1921 simply as Muljono, the son of a village headman in an obscure Central Javanese hamlet called Nginggil, Mbah Suro ended life forty-six years later where it began, but in a blaze of glory as several hundred crack government troops moved in during a dawn raid to put an end to his occult powers. His full title at the time of his death was the Most August Reverend Elder Mbah Suro – far more fitting for the self-styled 'saviour' of thousands that he had by then become. His steady rise to fame followed upon his success as a soothsayer during the fifties. By the early sixties, he had also attained recognition as a 'holy man', and acquired a growing band of youthful supporters who helped with the more commercial side of the business and acted as body-guards. When following the *coup,* these were joined by a few communist refugees, and increasing numbers among his followers began carrying guns (instead of magically endowed clubs) and allegedly promoting the causes of Sukarno and the Communist Party, authorities in Jakarta grew distinctly alarmed, and decided to put an end to his activities. In the aftermath, the military commander of neighbouring East Java decided to ban all forms of spiritualism which were 'considered contrary to the 1945 Constitution'. The commander also outlawed certain popular books on mysticism, and called upon followers of Mbah Suro in his region to hand in their potent talismans as a contribution for a public bonfire. But it would be idle to imagine that the episode spelt the end of mysticism and magic in Central and East Java.

Even so, the supernatural powers harnessed by modern-day Mbah Suros scarcely compare with the might of the 'god-kings' of the former famous Indonesian dynasties. In a fusion of native animism and Hindu and Buddhist beliefs, the king projected himself as a reincarnation of divinity, and the earthly focus of the mysterious 'life-force' animating all things. Others enjoyed authority only as a consequence of their nearness to the throne, since power – like the ripples from a pebble tossed into a pond – ebbed outward in ever weakening circles from the 'god-king'. In this way, Indian culture must have flooded many indigenous communities with fresh life and vitality, and probably, as Geertz believes, made 'kings out of chiefs, towns out of villages, and temples out of spirit houses'. And the resulting metamorphosis gave Indonesia more than a heritage of illustrious art, literature and architecture, such as Borobudur and the Prambanan temple complex. It also bequeathed an enduring social and political legacy through enshrining ideas, attitudes and values that have persisted into the present.

Not a few contemporary Indonesian leaders have tried to tread the same paths to power as their illustrious forbears. Sukarno, for instance, did little to discourage the belief among the Balinese people that he was the reincarnation of the Indian god Vishnu, but the way he exploited traditional beliefs to butress his authority will be considered more fully in the following chapter. Others have not always aimed quite so high. Often it has been enough just to capitalize on the paternalistic authoritarianism, the preoccupation with status and prestige, the fatalistic acceptance of man's 'lot', and the fascination for magically suggestive symbolism and ceremony that Javanese notions of man and society encourage.

In theory, the religion of Daud Beureueh should have ended all this – but that was not to be. After gaining a foothold in northern Sumatra by the end of the thirteenth century, Islam gradually spread throughout the archipelago until today it is nominally the faith of about ninety per cent of the Indonesian people. But as a liberating force, it was less than a universal success. It proved a useful weapon among Javanese underlords anxious to free themselves from the octopus-like grasp of the Madjapahit – the last and greatest of the Hindu-Javanese dynasties – since it challenged the authority of the 'god-king'. And it also fell upon fertile soil among matriarchal societies in Atjeh and West Sumatra, giving man a status he hitherto had lacked under village *adat*. But Islam's liberating message that man was no mere pawn in some vast cosmic chess game, but a special creature of God with a unique intelligence and capacity to help shape the world in which he lived, largely fell on deaf ears. Traditional village authority was reluctant to relinquish its hold over the people, so that only a minority of Indonesians professing Islam were truly 'born again' in the sense that Daud Beureueh recounts above. And millions of Javanese were especially reluctant to abandon their richly imaginative, intimate mythology for the stark loneliness of man confronting his creator across a seemingly vast chasm of space. Thus the result was often a 'marriage of convenience' between old beliefs and the new whereby the 'statistical' or nominal Muslim emerged. Or as the distinguished Indonesian diplomat and scholar Sudjatmoko so aptly notes, the Islamization of Indonesia was 'never actually fully consummated'.

Nonetheless, Islam has not yet abandoned the fight. During the struggle for independence in the earlier part of this century, the people were divided between those wanting to establish an Islamic state (like Daud Beureueh) and those favouring a secular state (like Sukarno). The outcome was a compromise – neither quite one nor the other – which has kept hopes alive among more orthodox Muslims that ultimately their objective of an Islamic state will be achieved. In turn, this has helped perpetuate the most long-standing and deep-seated schism within Indonesian society, so that, as Sudjatmoko observes, the 'shape of Indonesia's problems, and the priorities to be given to particular problems look different according to whether one's perspective and preoccupations are those of the Islamic historical experience or those of traditional Java'.

By the eve of the October 1965 *coup,* however, neither the Javanese way of life nor the Islamic looked liked triumphing as Sukarno promoted his revolutionary causes both domestically and abroad. Instead, the most dynamic social force emerging within Indonesia – the Communist Party – was inspired by the ideology of Marxism-Leninism, and aspirations not unlike those of Lai Pa Ka.

Even so, it should be stressed that Indonesia is not all diversity: it has its unifying threads. The common origin of most of the people has already been pointed out. Most of the 250 or so languages spoken by the people belong to the same linguistic family. And religious, cultural and economic patterns have united as well as divided during the more recent centuries as improved communications and technological advances have gradually brought the once scattered communities into closer contact. There is also the shared experience of colonial rule, and the struggle for independence, reinforced by the development of a national language (since the late twenties) and the unifying efforts of political leaders, and especially Sukarno, since the Republic was proclaimed.

Nor am I trying to suggest that the archipelago's diversity makes unity impossible. To do so would certainly be wrong. However, I have found a tendency among Westerners who have not had an opportunity to visit Indonesia to think of it much as they might their own national states. There is also a tendency among many Indonesians to pretend they are much more united than is really the case, and that their differences, when admitted, are not so important. These are among the tendencies I am trying to counteract, for I believe they give rise to false impressions, and encourage misunderstandings.

In his autobiography, Sukarno recalls his thoughts as he flew to Saigon early in August 1945 for talks with the Supreme Commander of all Japanese forces in Southeast Asia about Indonesia's future in the face of Japanese defeat by the Allied forces[1]. He ticked off the requirements of an independent nation-state. He noted the need for a country, a people, a government and another nation willing to accord recognition. Since the proclamation of their independence, barely a week later, the Indonesian people have been learning the hard way – as all nation-states must – that it is one thing to draw up a constitution, have one's national boundaries recognized under international law, and take a seat in the United Nations, and quite

1. Sukarno, *An Autobiography*. As told to Cindy Adams, Bobbs-Merrill, New York, 1965, p. 205.

another to translate these aspirations for nationhood into reality.

Effective government entails the will and skill to secure power as well as the ability to exercise it. Not only must a government convince a sufficient majority of people of its right to rule – unless it tries to govern with naked force – but also of the appropriateness of its policies, and especially its capacity to carry them out. Parliamentary democracy failed in the fifties on all these counts because too many political interests saw it as an alien system that did not represent their interests and aims, while promoting the position of their opponents. Guided Democracy won wider support but performed feebly as a system capable of coping with the realities of power among the heterogeneous peoples of the archipelago. As a result, Indonesians are still trying to agree among themselves about the fundamentals of government – who should rule, and how, and what national goals the country should pursue.

Figures such as Girang Adjal, Daud Beureueh and Lai Pa Ka reflect the scope of their disagreement. Few Indonesians share the extreme views of the Baduis, but millions are still basically inclined towards an authoritarian, paternalistic government and the fatalistic acceptance of their 'lot' in an unchanging, tradition-oriented society. Others are just as determined that society should break free from its tradition-bound, myth-ridden past and assume a more cosmopolitan outlook under Islamic law. Still others are even more pragmatic and assertive in seeking social and economic reform.

Other issues have also contributed towards political turbulence in post-independent Indonesia. For instance, economic considerations often compound conflict between ethnic Javanese who form nearly fifty per cent of the population and other ethnic groups. The Atjehnese are not alone among the peoples of the Outer Islands deeply resentful over the way a Java-based central government has neglected their needs for economic development.

Several million Chinese share the concern of Lai Pa Ka about their future following spasmodic outbursts of anti-Chinese feeling. Civilian-military hostilities have deepened since the *coup*. And other regional and ethnic rivalries, and personal ambitions, add to the difficulty the Republic confronts in seeking a 'national identity' and a workable form of government.

In the long term, the very diversity of ideas, values, attitudes, outlooks, cultural levels and social forms found throughout the archipelago may well prove to be among the Indonesian people's greatest strengths. More immediately, however, such is the urgency and magnitude of the country's economic and social problems, the failure to establish effective government gravely threatens the Republic's continued existence.

Chapter 3

The Fall of Sukarno

As an aspiring nation-builder, the late President Sukarno had no peers among his fellow countrymen. He aimed foremost at giving his people a sense of pride in being Indonesian. He wanted to raise their self-esteem and self-confidence. He dreamed of a great Indonesian nation stretching from 'Sabang to Merauke'. Relentlessly, he stressed 'national spirit', 'national consciousness', and the 'unity and oneness of the nation'. To forge this 'oneness', and to 'feed the souls of the people', he whipped up revolutionary ardour among the masses, exploited real and imaginary enemies and crises, fashioned magical, mystical unifying formulas and symbols, promoted Guided Democracy, and poured billions of dollars of borrowed money into massive armed forces and grandiose prestige projects, asserting that these were 'as important to an Indonesian as his trousers'. However, while he did succeed in instilling in the people a sense of national pride they had previously lacked, his country was far from being a strong, united nation at the time of the attempted *coup d'état* of October 1965 – the event that precipitated his fall from power.

Probably no man will ever again dominate the Indonesian scene so completely as Sukarno did during the years preceding the attempted *coup*. President of the Republic of Indonesia, Mandatory of the People's Congress, Great Leader of the Revolution, the Mouthpiece of the Indonesian People, Chairman of the Supreme Operational Command, Great Leader of the Workers, Father of the Farmers, Highest Leader of the National Front, Caretaker of the Message of the People's Suffering, Supreme Commander of the Mental Revolution, Supreme Shepherd of the Women's Revolutionary Movement, Saviour of the

Nation, Lifetime Supreme Leader of the National Association of Football Clubs, Champion of Islam and Freedom, Supreme Scout, Prime Minister, His Most Exalted Excellency, the Honourable Doctor Engineer Hadji Raden Sukarno . . . to list but a few of the scores of titles and honours showered upon him during his lifetime. For he was the man who with no small measure of truth could slam his fist upon a table and angrily declare: 'Sukarno was the architect of this Republic. Sukarno is the founder and father and builder of this nation. Sukarno is the leader and President and Prime Minister of this country. Let nobody forget that.'

In his autobiography, Sukarno recounts how his birth in East Java in 1901, allegedly at the moment of sunrise, marked him out, according to Javanese belief, as a man destined for glory and greatness.[1] The gods were even supposed to have greeted baby Sukarno with the eruption of a nearby volcano, such was the import of his awakening hours. He also regarded himself fortunate to have been born under Gemini (his birthday was double six – 6 June) signifying a dual personality: poetic or hard as steel, gentle or exacting, a mixture of emotion and reason. He stressed his ruling class origins, though both parents were poor and unimportant. His mother, a Balinese, was of Hindu high caste (Brahmin), and of Balinese royal blood. His father, one of the countless titled Javanese, traced his lineage several centuries back into the past. Among millions of Javanese, Sukarno eventually gained great political capital through the myth spun about his 'portentous beginnings' and aristocratic ancestry. To many, he became a 'god-king', cast in the same mould as the rulers of the great Hindu-Javanese realms: omnipotent and omniscient, the fount of all earthly power, and the arbiter of all discord among his people. Their commitment to him was total and intimately interwoven with their innermost beliefs.

1. Sukarno, *An Autobiography*. As told to Cindy Adams, Bobbs-Merrill, New York, 1965, p. 17.

Sukarno's rise to power began in the late twenties in Bandung, West Java, where he studied for an engineering degree. In 1927, he helped found the Indonesian Nationalist Party (PNI), and his fame grew during the early thirties as a mounting wave of nationalist sentiment rolled through the archipelago. Although he wrote prolifically, he was never an especially profound and original thinker. His talent lay rather in his lively imagination, great vitality and evocative expression. He was a communicator without equal among his people, often giving tired old ideas new life. And perhaps most pertinently, he was an astute psychologist, shrewdly understanding the aspirations of his fellow countrymen. But as an orator, he especially excelled, stirring the hearts and souls of the downtrodden and dispirited. His imposing personality and presence, his authorative resonant voice, and his lucid, repetitive and persuasive presentations, captivated ever-increasing audiences, lifting him to the forefront of the country's popular political leaders.

After collaborating with the Japanese during the occupation, his name was a household word throughout Java, and beyond, but his position as a nationalist leader was compromised in the eyes of Allied powers. Although chosen by his colleagues as President of the Republic he had proclaimed on 17 August 1945, he was forced by domestic political events to remain in the background of Indonesian politics until the late fifties. He pulled strings behind the scenes, dextrously ensuring the success of his supporters and the defeat and downfall of recognizable rivals and opponents among both civilian and military circles. His activities aided the collapse of the parliamentary system of government, which gave him only limited powers as President. And as parliamentary democracy crumbled, he pressed for its replacement with his more truly 'Indonesian' alternative of Guided Democracy. With army backing, he established this system by decree on 5 July 1959, returning the Republic to the original 1945 Constitution (which gave wide powers to the Presidency but had been abandoned in the late forties), and continued his quest for greater power.

The dawning of Guided Democracy found Sukarno sharing power mainly with the army. His strength derived from his personal popularity and charismatic appeal. He held undisputed primacy as 'Leader of the Revolution' and the Republic's first and only President. He had no peers among his people as a skilled orator and political performer. And he had profited by seizing the initiative and formulating an alternative, acceptable form of government as parliamentary democracy floundered. On the other hand, the strength of the army stemmed from a virtual monopoly of physical force. It had gained great influence through the imposition of martial law early in 1957, and from the decisive and effective manner in which it had acted against regional rebellion, especially in view of the inability of the parliamentary system to cope with this challenge to central government authority and national unity. Of the residue of power still residing with the largely discredited political parties, only the Communist Party retained a position of any real consequence.

Between Sukarno and the army, a complex, ambivalent relationship emerged. They agreed on the past divisiveness of political parties, and on the need to reorder the state with a singleness of purpose and command. But even as Sukarno joined with the army in formally emasculating the power of the parties (through replacing the old institutions with the instruments of Guided Democracy), he began hedging against the possibility of himself becoming a captive of army power. For this he was able to exploit the general suspicion of civilian groups towards military involvement in political and economic affairs, divisions and rivalries within the army and confusion over its nonmilitary function, and especially the army's long-standing antagonism towards the Communist Party. During the ensuing years of Guided Democracy, these issues emerged as sources of domestic conflict, since control – or, at the very least, the co-operation – of military power was an essential requirement for ruling the heterogeneous, far-flung Indonesian island complex.

The army-Communist Party conflict dated back to the 1948 Madiun rebellion when communists and left-wing elements, including members of the military forces, had attempted to overthrow the Republican government even while the armed struggle was proceeding against the Dutch. In addition, suspicion and mistrust arose among some elements of the officer corps as a result of the Party's atheistic and international outlook. But the conflict deepened during the late fifties and early sixties since the Communist Party posed a rival threat to army power. For Sukarno, the conflict provided a means of compensating for his own lack of organized support, and offsetting his fears and suspicions that elements of the officer corps might try to impose military rule.

The army-Communist Party conflict came to a head during 1960 when some military commanders, antagonized by the Party's criticisms and alarmed by its growing strength, cracked down on its activities in their regions. Disregarding the military view of the growing threat of communism, Sukarno entered into a protracted struggle with anti-communist army leaders, seeking not only the revocation of all measures taken against the Communist Party, but also tighter controls over the political decisions of regional army commanders. While some of the bans were not lifted until late in 1961, and restrictions against the Party continued in the most strongly anti-communist (and pro-Muslim) regions of South Sumatra, South Sulawesi (Celebes) and South Kalimantan, the army lost the 'test of strength'.

Because of their diverse ethnic, religious, social and educational backgrounds, and their deep political involvement, army officers differed among themselves on many major issues, including the position of Sukarno in the power structure, his policies in general, and his support for the Communist Party. By playing one faction off against another, or appealing to the loyalty of certain

officers he assiduously courted, Sukarno gradually under-
mined the authority of the more 'independent-minded'
and anti-communist officers within the corps. His major
'coup' was the 'promotion' of General A. H. Nasution
to the newly created post of Chief of Staff of the Armed
Forces late in June 1962. Nasution had been a dominating
influence in the army since the early years of its formation, and had clashed with Sukarno on a number of occasions. Sumatran born, and a devout Muslim, his whole
outlook on life contrasted sharply with that of the flam-
boyant Sukarno. Nasution wanted a strong, independent
army, fully behind the President as the nation's foremost
leader, but able to influence his policies and actions.
Sukarno wanted a much more compliant army leadership
prepared to carry out his orders without question. The
creation of the post of Chief of Staff of the Armed Forces
was originally intended by Nasution and others to be a
major step towards the unification of the four military
services – the army, navy, air force and police. Sukarno
made sure that the real power remained with the individual service commanders, and that Nasution's new post
had little more than a tiresome administrative function.
Sukarno was able to do this largely because the navy, air
force and police feared army domination in any united
command.

In his hold over the country, Sukarno had a further
weapon which he proceeded to wield with increasing
vigour. Through Guided Democracy, he had gained a
monopoly of the formulation and inculcation of state
ideology. His speech, 'The Rediscovery of Our Revolution', delivered as the independence day address in August
1959, soon formed the core of the 'Political Manifesto of
the Republic of Indonesia' (MANIPOL). And that was
just a beginning of a finely spun web of ideological and
institutional commitment in which Sukarno skilfully ensnared the Indonesian people, including army leaders, and
ensured their loyalty through the threat of being branded
'counter-revolutionaries' and traitors to the Republic.

USDEK, RE-SO-PIM, NASAKOM, TAVIP, and others, followed in quick succession. USDEK was the acronym coined for the essence of MANIPOL: the 1945 Constitution, Guided Democracy, Guided Economy, Indonesian Socialism and the Indonesian Identity. RE-SO-PIM – Revolution, Indonesian Socialism and the National Leadership – stressed an essential and inseparable trinity by which Sukarno's role as 'Great Leader of the Indonesian Revolution' was instilled with a mystical, inviolable legitimacy. NASAKOM assured nationalist, religious and communist forces of a 'place in the Indonesian sun'. TAVIP prodded the faint-hearted and exhorted all to 'live dangerously' late in 1964 when the Sukarno magic showed signs of losing momentum, and so on. Each, according to Sukarno was a different kind of 'instrument' for 'equipping and rounding out' the political unity of the nation.

At the heart of his ideological underpinning of Indonesian society was the notion of 'Indonesian-ness'. According to Sukarno, Guided Democracy was not just another system of government, but the 'rediscovery of the treasury of the Indonesian people which has lain buried during hundreds of years of foreign rule'. It recognized an idealized version of the traditional village as the source of Indonesian 'identity', and the corner-stone of the growth of national policy, culture and economy. It affirmed the traditional village political processes of *musjawarat* (consultations or discussions), *mupakat* (agreement), *gotong rojong* (mutual co-operation). And the Constitution on which the Republic rested was supposed to reflect this ancient heritage from Indonesia's 'beautiful past'. Sukarno, who revelled in the role of national 'elder', and playing the 'Big *Bapak*' (Big Father), explained the idea this way in 1959:

The 1945 Constitution is the genuine reflection of the identity of the Indonesian people, who since ancient times based their system of government *musjawarat* and *mupakat* with the leadership of one central authority in the hands of a 'sesepuh' — an elder — who did not dictate, but led, and protected. Indonesian democracy since ancient times has been Guided Democracy, and this is the characteristic of all original democracies in Asia.[1]

And unlike the divisive, Western democratic concept of 'one man, one vote', decision making in the Indonesian system did not involve a contest between opposing views, resolutions and counter-resolutions, and the taking of sides, but only a 'persistent effort to find common ground in solving a problem'. From such a system, Sukarno asserted, flowed the kind of 'tomorrow' for which he knew millions of his countrymen yearned – and here he would often use a Javanese phrase roughly meaning 'order, peace, joyous labour, prosperity, fertility, whatever you plant will grow, whatever you buy is cheap'.

Not all Indonesians found this version of 'Indonesian-ness' and national 'identity' to their liking. Both the language and values betrayed an essentially Javanese bias. And in Sukarno's life-style and political appeal were distinct echoes of the 'god-king' and the past glory of the Javanese realm. Increasingly, he projected himself into a role transcending the ordinary domain of domestic politics. Appearing to remain aloof from sordid power squabbles, he asserted his supremacy as arbiter of all disputes and interpreter of all doctrines. He had the title of 'President' reserved for himself, and early in 1963, during a conference of governors in the history-steeped Central Javanese city of Solo, was accorded the title of 'Grand Elder', traditionally reserved for great kings. And gradually his personality and presence so dominated the country and people that he could boast that 'Sukarno alone is the cohesive factor in Indonesia. After I'm gone the only cement to hold the islands together will be their national pride.' Like France's Louise XIV, and the Javanese kings

1. *Political Manifesto Republic of Indonesia of 17 August 1959*, Department of Information, Jakarta, Special Issue 53, p. 62.

of old, Sukarno had become so closely equated with the State, he might well have added: *'L'Etat c'est moi.'*

Such an approach offered several political advantages. Not only did the tradition-dominated Javanese constitute the most ready-made political majority throughout the archipelago, but also offered greater opportunities for exercising political control. His own popularity, and the support of his two most dependent political allies, the Communist Party and the Nationalist Party were firmly rooted among these people. The Javanese also dominated the Indonesian bureaucracy and comprised about three-quarters of the officers in the army. Further, their position had been markedly strengthened by the failure of the rebellion in Sumatra and Sulawesi (Celebes) during the late fifties. Among the values and attitudes of the Javanese way of life on which Sukarno could also capitalize were the stress on harmony and unity within the community and the avoidance of overt conflict. Another advantage was the capacity of the people to accommodate a broad spectrum of beliefs and viewpoints. Unlike orthodox Muslims, for example, they were not so intolerant of other beliefs. Moreover, through allusions to the concept of the 'god-king', and the mystique of symbols and ceremony, Sukarno could become less dependent on concrete achievement as a basis of his legitimacy, at least, among large numbers of simple Javanese peasants.

Most dissenters were speedily silenced. Hostility to his teachings was equated with treachery. Newspapers had the choice of actively promoting state ideology or having their licences revoked. Journalists were obliged to attend indoctrination courses where objective reporting was roundly condemned. Only news favouring the 'revolution' was fit to print. Likewise political rivals were imprisoned without trial, forced to flee the country, or retire into self-imposed, ignominious silence. The disillusioned socialist leader, Sutan Sjahrir, Muslim leaders like Muhammad Roem, Prawoto Mangkusasmito and Muhammad Natsir, and the author-publisher, Mochtar Lubis, were but a few of the distinguished Indonesian leaders kept under detention. The noted economist, Dr Sumitro Djojohadikusumo, was among those who chose exile abroad. But these were mainly the more Westernized socialist and Islamic elements of the national leadership: men who were least in sympathy with Sukarno's idea of Indonesian 'identity' and his policies and priorities for the nation.

Even so, despite the public acclaim Sukarno generally enjoyed, all was not well within the kingdom. Increasingly, he found himself contending with what he called the 'two-faced MANIPOLlist', the 'fake MANIPOLlist' – the opponent who publicly acknowledged the 'king', but privately plotted his overthrow. Increasingly, therefore, the real power struggle in the critical period preceding the October 1965 attempted *coup* took place behind the scenes with the public glimpsing only the shadows of reality as the contestants – mainly the army, the Communist Party and Sukarno – jockeyed within a vaguely felt set of 'rules of the game', scrupulously trying to preserve an outward appearance of great unity and purpose.

This 'power game' which Guided Democracy encouraged was a notably complex affair. Opponents usually only publicly expressed disagreement in oblique and ambiguous terms. Lengthy negotiations and discussions frequently ended in the misleading appearance that agreement had been reached, when, in fact, the conflict had only been postponed and prolonged rather than resolved. Often too, concessions made during negotiations were only token commitments, never likely to be honoured. Such was *musjawarat* and *mupakat* in practice, as distinct from the ideal. Devious rather than direct tactics were favoured to undermine and weaken opponents. Criticisms and ridicule through innuendo and hyperbole, the exploitation of rivalries and jealousies, and the dissemination of suspicion and unrest through spreading rumours and dubious 'information' were also popular ruses.

The 'power game' was also noted for the formation of

fleeting alliances and counter-alliances. Frequently, these cut across the three main social forces – nationalist, religious and communist – which Sukarno recognized with his NASAKOM formula for Indonesian unity. They were mostly tenuous marriages-of-convenience formed for pragmatic rather than ideological or even social and economic reasons. Factions tentatively probed and tested each other's strength, but few contests were fought to a conclusive finish. Before the 'point of no return' in any contest had arisen, usually one party or group would have given way and retired to await a more suitable opportunity for pursuing its objectives. As such, the system favoured the skilful exponent of psychological warfare, and consequently was often characterized by wide discrepancies between actual and presumed power. In general, contestants also tried to avoid making the first public move, so that others might assume responsibility for any public discord that emerged. The American scholar Ann Ruth Willner believes that this 'power game' was probably not unlike the statecraft practised in the courts of the traditional Javanese kings.

For the army leadership, the 'power game' increasingly became a question of survival. During the early sixties, Sukarno led an all-out campaign for the recovery of West Irian (formerly West New Guinea), which the Dutch had persistently refused to even talk about, let alone cede, since transferring sovereignty over the rest of their former colony to the Republic in 1949. Using the issue as 'proof' that the Indonesian 'revolution' had not been completed (an issue he had publicly debated with former Vice President Muhammad Hatta in the mid-fifties), and that the struggle against 'imperialism and colonialism' must be stepped up, Sukarno declared the territory would be taken by force, if necessary. The campaign admirably suited his agitational skills, and its highly successful conclusion in August 1962 lifted him to a new peak of popularity and pre-eminence among his people. Likewise the Communist Party also made the most of the opportunities the campaign gave it to organize, demonstrate and expand. But the army fared less happily, despite the massive purchases of arms (which mainly went to the air force and navy). Army leaders like Nasution had entered the campaign rather half-heartedly, believing other issues such as national security and the worsening economic situation deserved more urgent attention. Then the major part played by diplomacy took the edge from the military role. As a result, the army emerged as a far less potent political force in Indonesian society than it had been at the beginning of Guided Democracy, and its power looked like declining even further with the ending of martial law in May 1963.

When Sukarno next turned to 'confronting' the proposed Malaysian federation, the army soon found itself in more trouble. As with the West Irian campaign, Malaysian confrontation evoked a turbulent domestic climate that damaged army cohesion and promoted the position of Sukarno and the Communist Party. As the country's economy continued to decline through neglect and reckless fiscal policy (inflation during 1962 was the worst the Republic had ever experienced, and continued to climb by leaps and bounds during the following years), the army leadership found itself committed to a war it could not win, while morale among the troops was falling and the Communist Party seemed to be forging ahead. By the later part of 1964, the Communist Party was claiming more than 3 million members, and about 16 million others in affiliated organizations under its control. Such was the Party's burgeoning growth, some observers believed it was well along the road to assuming power by 'default' or 'acclamation'. And to make matters worse for the army, under the banner of the 'new emerging forces' and the struggle to 'build the world anew', Sukarno was leading Indonesia into a closer alignment with Peking, which could hardly fail to promote the power of the Communist Party even further.

In appropriate 'power game' style, the army leadership

responded to the challenge by covertly 'cooling' the war with Malaysia in the latter months of 1964, and sending out guarded 'peace feelers' through secret contacts abroad. Such were the intricacies of these manoeuvres that the most senior army officer who took part in the attempted *coup*, Brigadier General Supardjo, commented during his trial that 'we cannot say the army leadership opposed confrontation . . . [but] we felt that things were not being done whole-heartedly, and that the effort was even being sabotaged'. Among other things, the army leadership ensured that key troops fell under the command of officers they could trust. Supardjo, who was not among these, found himself 'waiting' for most of the troops intended for his command on the Malaysian front.

Nonetheless, Sukarno, aided by the Communist Party, continued to apply pressure on the army leadership during 1965. Through withdrawing from the United Nations, accepting economic aid from Peking, and stressing 'self-reliance', he sought, among other aims, to heighten the Indonesian people's sense of isolation and physical threat. Through playing on rivalries and divisions within the army, and between the military services, he sought also to further weaken the influence of conservative elements within the military leadership. Through political indoctrination and pressure from some political parties to introduce political commissars into the army, concerted efforts were also made to create a 'people's army' more directly and firmly under civilian control. Other efforts were directed towards the formation of a 'fifth force' by arming 'revolutionary' peasants and workers, and thereby diluting the army's monopoly of physical force. Thus, through a process of attrition, Sukarno hoped that the less 'revolutionary' among the army leadership would either change their outlook, or be replaced by others more responsive to the 'Presidential will'.

Among the other armed services, these tactics met with considerable success. Early in March 1965, a revolt within the navy of about 700 officers calling themselves the 'revolutionary progressive officers' movement' succeeded in seriously undermining the authority of the moderate navy commander, Rear Admiral E. Martadinata, though they failed to bring about his dismissal. Similarly, revolutionary pressures plagued and divided the police. And under Air Vice Marshal Omar Dani, the air force was already completely under Sukarno's sway, and enjoyed close relations with the Communist Party. This trend within the services was part of the 'crystallization' of the 'forces of the Indonesian revolution' which Sukarno regarded as necessary to bring about the development of a united, dynamic Republic.

Even so, the army leadership continued to parry thrusts made against its autonomy. It headed off initial attempts by the Communist Party to get the 'workers and peasants' armed by giving strongly anti-communist workers in Sumatra some weapons. It came out of a long and tortuous debate with the Communist Party over the meaning of NASAKOM with an assertion that 'political commissars' would not be included in the army 'now or in the future because the army already had its foundations, namely *Pantja Sila,* and army personnel were real NASAKOMists as a result of *Pantja Sila* feeling'! It also countered proposals for a 'fifth force' by arguing that as long as Indonesia (unlike China) still had 'nine or ten powerful political parties, each with its own ideology and objectives' there could be no guarantee that arming peasants and workers would not 'lead to undesirable consequences'. And through all this, everyone – ally and opponent – vigorously asserted loyalty to Sukarno, dedication to Guided Democracy, determination in the struggle to 'crush' Malaysia, and resolution as a beacon among the 'new emerging forces'.

By this stage, however, the army leadership had grown distinctly more divided and confused. Its power had been dispersed, but not subordinated to civilian control. Within army headquarters, a small group of mainly Javanese officers clustered around the commander of the army,

Lieutenant General Achmad Yani. Yani had succeeded to the post when Nasution moved into the newly created position of Chief of Staff of the Armed Forces in June 1962. Another very small group of officers within the Army's Strategic Reserve Command (KOSTRAD), which had control over all army troops involved in the Malaysian campaign, looked more to their own commander, Major General Suharto, who was later to succeed to the Presidency through the turn of events. Still others were more readily identifiable as supporters of General Nasution. They were all anti-communist, but differed in their attitude towards Sukarno and the system of Guided Democracy towards corruption and inefficiency, towards the 'revolution', the Communist Party, and the role of the armed forces in the political sphere. Other anti-communist military leaders such as Major General Ibrahim Adjie, then commanding the influential Siliwangi (West Java) corps, and prominent figures among the Diponegoro (Central Java) and Brawidjaja (East Java) corps were more committed to Sukarno for personal reasons. And at the other end of the spectrum were the extreme radical and pro-communist officers, such as the East Indonesian Inter-Regional Commander, Major General Rukman, and Colonel A. Sjukur, a lecturer at the Army Staff and Command School (SESKOAD), Bandung. In brief, these favoured the changes Sukarno and the Communist Party were urging upon the army, but they were only on the fringes of army power and were consistently out-voted by the more conservative elements within the officer corps. However, these differences all came to a head with the attempted *coup*.

The broad outlines of what happened on 1 October 1965 are now fairly well known. In co-ordinated pre-dawn raids, armed squads kidnapped six senior army generals, but a seventh on their list, General Nasution, escaped. Other troops seized control of vital installations, such as the radio and telecommunications networks. [The troops involved included one company from the élite Presidential guard, the Tjakrabirawa Regiment, two battalions of army paracommandos from Central and East Java, which were in Jakarta for the 5 October armed forces' anniversary parade, one battalion of air force paracommandos, two platoons of infantry troops from the Jakarta garrison, and about 2,000 youths with limited military training. Facilities for training the youths (mainly drawn from communist and left-wing organizations), and for launching the raids on the houses of the generals, were provided by the air force at Halim air base on the outskirts of Jakarta]. For most Indonesians, first news of the events came through an early morning radio broadcast a few hours after the abduction of the generals. Listeners were told that a military operation, the 'September 30 Movement' ('solely a movement within the army') had acted against the self-styled Council of Generals' – a 'subversive body sponsored by the United States' Central Intelligence Agency' which had been 'very active lately, especially since President Sukarno was seriously ill in the first week of August this year'. As leader of the 'Movement', Lieutenant Colonel Untung, a battalion commander of the President's personal bodyguard, the Tjakrabirawa Regiment, had recognized his 'duty to protect the President' from the generals who were planning a 'counter-revolutionary' *coup*. Declared the broadcast:

Power-mad generals and officers who have neglected the lot of their men and who above the accumulated sufferings of their men have lived in luxury, led a gay life, insulted our women and wasted government funds, must be kicked out of the army and punished accordingly. The army is not for generals, but is the possession of all the soldiers of the army who are loyal to the ideals of the Revolution of August 1945 . . . [1]

In later broadcasts, the 'Movement' declared Sukarno's cabinet defunct, and named a forty-five member Revolution Council as the 'source of all authority in the Republic

1. See the 'Initial Statement of Lieutenant Colonel Untung', *Indonesia*, vol. 1, April 1966, Ithaca, New York, p. 135.

of Indonesia', pending general elections. Council members included a broad cross-section of the country's ruling élite, notably excluding strongly anti-communist leaders and favouring 'Sukarnoists' and communist supporters and sympathizers. Three of the forty-five (twenty-three civilians and twenty-two military) were known communists, but none was of heavyweight calibre. During the afternoon, Sukarno was reported as safe and well, but his whereabouts was not disclosed.

Throughout the day, the general situation remained highly confused. By 8 p.m., however, the broadcasting studio had passed to the control of counter-*coup* forces led by the KOSTRAD commander, Major General Suharto, and shortly before 9 p.m., the army began broadcasting its version of events. With equal vigour the army professed loyalty to 'Bung Karno (Sukarno) as the Great Leader of the Revolution', and told of a 'counter-revolutionary' movement which had kidnapped Lieutenant General Achmad Yani, the army commander, Major Generals Suprapto, S. Parman and Harjono, and Brigadier Generals D. I. Pandjaitan and Sutojo Siswomihardjo. Both the President and General Nasution, however, were 'able to be brought to safety and are in a safe and well condition'. The announcement said that Major General Suharto was temporarily in command of the army, and that the 'general situation is again under control and security measures are being actively carried out'. A statement authorized by Suharto added: 'By establishing what they called an Indonesian Revolution Council, and by declaring the cabinet defunct, it became obvious they (Movement) were counter-revolutionaries committing a *coup* against the President . . . besides kidnapping several high-ranking army officers.'

Following the *coup*, there was far from universal agreement as to how these events and assertions should be interpreted. Some still maintain, though their ranks have grown thin, that the *coup* was more or less what Untung had claimed – an 'internal army affair', reflecting serious tension between 'high living', corrupt officers of the central command and the lower ranking officers and ordinary ranks. Others accept the argument of the army leadership, with varying reservations, that the events were masterminded and directed by the Communist Party from behind the scenes.

The army has built its case largely around an obscure figure called Sjam. He was not captured until early in March 1967, and four months later, appeared for the first time in court during the trial of the communist leader, Sudisman. He gave his name as Kamarusaman bin Achmad Mubaidah, and admitted to a string of aliases including Sjam. He said he was born in April 1924 at Tuban, East Java, and had been a member of the Communist Party since 1949. He had served an apprenticeship in youth and labour organizations, and, in 1957, had graduated to the personal staff of the Chairman of the Communist Party, D. N. Aidit. From 1960, he had been in charge of a section dealing with party members among the armed forces, and in November 1964, was given the task of forming a secret organization, the 'special bureau', for the purpose of winning party support among senior officers of the armed forces. From this position, Sjam claimed, acting under Aidit's orders, he had master-minded the *coup*.

According to the army version, the events of the *coup* were triggered off by Sukarno's dramatic illness early in August 1965. Sukarno had collapsed, and, for a while, seemed to be seriously ill. The army claim that Aidit feared a further attack could lead to the paralysis or death of the President. (Aidit allegedly received this information from Chinese doctors who were treating Sukarno at the time). To avoid army repression in the possibly imminent post-Sukarno period, the army argues, the Communist Party decided to remove the most obstructive anti-communist army leaders from power, and generally (through the formation of the Indonesian Revolution Council) move the political constellation towards the left, paving the way for the still unrealized NASAKOM government. And to prevent arousing the still not inconsiderable anti-communist feeling within the country's ruling circles, the Communist Party tried to capitalize on discontent within the officer corps – which it had helped generate through the activities of Sjam's 'special bureau' – by presenting the *coup* as an 'internal army affair', and ensuring that leading communist figures and organizations were kept well out of sight. Consequently, the army asserts, the *coup* was not a direct communist bid for power but a strategy by which the Party could continue its upward climb.

Despite certain unsatisfactory aspects of the army version, it is far more plausible than the bland claim of the *coup* leaders that the matter was simply an 'internal army affair'. The weight of evidence is clearly to the contrary, indicating that a far wider circle of interests had a stake in the outcome of events. Whether Aidit through Sjam actually set the *coup* wheels turning may still be open to dispute, but there can be little doubt that Aidit and other Communist Party leaders were involved. Among the Party's top four or five leaders, only Sudisman survived the army purge following the *coup*. During his trial, he admitted he was involved as an 'individual' but denied that the Party, as a whole, was involved, arguing that the matter had never been discussed at a full session of the Party's central committee. In view of Aidit's autocratic hold over the Party, army leaders find such distinctions too much like splitting hairs. And there are reasons for believing that Aidit felt confident the *coup*, as planned, could have succeeded without widespread party involvement.

Whether or not the army leadership itself was planning a *coup* doubtless will never be known. It certainly had cause enough to be concerned about the growing power of the Community Party and its own confusion, but reasons also for not assuming the initiative. Even so, the army has been less than frank about many of its activities before the *coup*. It has avoided disclosing details of secret contacts with Malaysia begun late in 1964, and of secret missions to Kuala Lumpur early in 1965. It has failed to establish the authorship of the so-called 'Gilchrist letter' (a top secret cable former British Ambassador Gilchrist allegedly sent his superior in London in March 1965 which infers that army generals were working in cohorts with the United States and Britain to unseat Sukarno) though it asserts the 'letter' was a forgery. And the report of an army appointed committee hastily set up following the *coup* to quash rumours about the 'Council of Generals' skates around the real issues in an highly unconvincing fashion, and has since been contradicted by evidence arising during the trials of those implicated in the *coup*. And these are just a few of the hazy aspects of the army's explanation of events which will continue to cast doubts upon the credibility of its overall claims.

As for Sukarno's role, this also will probably remain a mystery. It is hard to believe he did not know broadly what was in the wind. He may even have indirectly encouraged the *coup* by privately indicating his displeasure with the army leadership, perhaps in the vein of 'who will rid me of those meddlesome priests?' At least, there is little doubt where his heart lay, having later called the episode a 'ripple in the ocean of the revolution'. And he did decide to go to Halim air base on the morning of the *coup* when the outcome of events was still unclear. But it is doubtful whether he would have wanted to have known too much detail before the event. Otherwise, his own position could have become quickly compromised. And it is quite possible that in declaring his cabinet defunct and forming an Indonesian Revolution Council (which did not include his name), the *coup* leaders went beyond the action he would have been prepared to endorse. 'Are you crazy?' he later claimed he told *coup* leaders on learning that they had set up the council. 'Are you crazy to think that I would allow my cabinet to be declared defunct?' But most probably, Sukarno alone knew the full extent of his involvement, and this knowledge, no doubt, he carried to his grave when he died on 21 June 1970, a lonely, disappointed man.

Throughout his life, Sukarno followed a simple formula for implanting nationalism among his people. 'There are three steps,' he had argued in the early thirties. 'Firstly, we show the people that their past was a beautiful past; secondly, we add to the people's awareness that their present is a dark present; thirdly, we show the people a shining future, and the way to reach this future full of promise.' It was in showing his people the way to reach their 'shining future' that Sukarno took the road to Halim, only to discover it led to a dead end.

Sukarno believed the way to achieve an Indonesian 'tomorrow' was through organizing forces that were capable of being carried along by an idea. What that idea was – independence, a 'new world', and so on, – almost seemed to be of secondary importance. Nor did he deny the need for schools, hospitals, factories and other concrete, material achievements, but these, he believed, should be given a lesser priority to the task of 'creating spirit, creating awareness, creating hope, creating ideology', or what he called the 'spiritual artillery' of the nation.

Under Guided Democracy, Sukarno disregarded the pressing economic needs of his people. He created a highly personal, impotent form of government, that may have resembled the courts of the ancient Javanese kings, but was ill-suited to the demands of the twentieth century. He did demonstrate the tremendous political potential of traditional forces in Indonesian society, but he failed to show how those forces could be harnessed to the cause of providing a better future for his people. And he miscalculated the real depth of their differences. He believed that upon the forges of 'revolution', he could fashion a NASAKOM unity from their diversity. Events proved otherwise: the power of the army proved irreconcilable with that of the Communist Party. And the attempted *coup* dramatically underlined his ultimate failure as a nation-builder. It also paved the way for the rise of the army to power, and a different approach to achieving a brighter future for the Indonesian people.

Chapter 4

The Rise of the Army

There is no simple way to describe the Indonesian National Army (TNI) as a political force. Its officers come from varying ethnic, religious, social and educational backgrounds, although about three-quarters are Javanese, and most were recruited from the lower aristocracy or better educated social groups. A very few had received Dutch military training before the independence struggle. Most probably gained their first training from the Japanese during World War II. Some began as members of armed student corps or politically aligned guerrilla forces formed during the war against the Dutch in the late forties. Still others were trained in the post-independence period. But most claim they enlisted as 'patriots' rather than 'career' military men, and their political claims are centred on their long involvement in 'safeguarding' the Republic. 'When Sukarno ran up the white flag (in Jogjakarta, Central Java, when the Dutch overran the town in 1948), and when the Dutch arrested the cabinet ministers, the Republic *was* the army – just a bunch of armed men,' a distinguished officer, Major General Mokoginta, told me in 1969. 'Time and again, the army has come to the rescue of the Republic – during the fifties, and again in the sixties. That is why we insist on a say, insist on being consulted ...'

Accounts of the army generally argue that the varied backgrounds of the officers prevented the development of a non-political, united, professional army. Unity was also impaired by physical and organizational problems, such as geography, lack of communications and the failure of the national leadership to overcome the autonomous nature of many military units formed during the struggle against the Dutch. However, a German scholar, Ulf Sund-haussen, who spent two years (1967-8) interviewing army officers in Indonesia, argues that studies so far lack sufficient depth to provide a satisfactory understanding of the army as a political force. Too often, the military has been treated only marginally, and mainly as a disruptive force, in post-independence Indonesian events, while little or no attempt has been made to examine the backgrounds of the officers, their ideological commitments, or the structure and organization of the army and the other armed services.

In an unpublished thesis, 'The Development of Political Orientation and Involvement of the Indonesian Army Officer Corps: The Case Study of the Siliwangi Division', (Monash University), Sundhaussen claims most officers were not basically hostile towards civilian authority at the beginning of independence. What changed their attitude was the negligence, obstruction and provocation of civilian authority towards the army. A more sensible attitude on the part of the politicians, a more realistic appraisal of army values, and a better performance by parliament (in the fifties) could have kept the army from moving into civilian jobs, he asserts.

Firstly, Sundhaussen believes, civilian leaders bungled the establishment of the armed forces. Initially, they supported the disarmament of units formed by the Japanese during the occupation. Then, after deciding to form a defence organization, they failed to give it proper attention. When the officers themselves tried to bring some order to their early chaos, they met with government obstruction. During the fifties, at no stage did successive civilian governments provide adequate funds for even the military's basic needs, such as food, housing and a very low salary. Lacking money, local army commanders were forced to find other ways of financing their needs, and increasingly turned to smuggling, corruption and extortion. While undoubtedly some officers made handsome personal profits from these activities, it was, nonetheless, civilian authority that initially forced them into corrupt practices.

Even more serious, was civilian meddling in military matters. During the first three years of the armed struggle against the Dutch, the government maintained irregular forces over which regular army commanders could exercise no control even during military operations. And while the majority of officers were highly nationalistic Javanese, the government first appointed a Christian Sumatran with extreme left-wing political views as the Republic's first defence minister. When following the transfer of sovereignty in 1950 the army leadership attempted to modernize and professionalize the army through demobilization, education and training, parliament thwarted these plans. While certain army leaders may have over-reacted in October 1952 when they tried to force Sukarno to assume more direct leadership of the Republic, Sundhaussen claims they were justified in concluding that the politicians held party and personal interest above those of the nation. Finally, officers resolved in the 1955 'Jogjakarta Declaration', among other things, to resist further civilian interference in strictly military matters.

One of the officers involved in the attempt to have Sukarno assume greater powers, and disband the existing parliament, in October 1952, was General Nasution. At the time he was Chief of Staff of the Army, with the rank of Colonel, and was forced to resign his post when the ill-conceived plan misfired. During an interview in 1969, Nasution told me that after his dismissal, he had concluded that the 'duality' between the political and military leadership both during the independence struggle and also in the early fifties had been very harmful for the Republic. He also concluded that only by reviving the 'spirit of the '45 struggle', and reuniting the 'revolutionary forces' could this division be healed. When he was reappointed to the post of Chief of Staff of the Army in 1955, he began working towards these objectives.

During the latter part of the fifties, events such as the

proclamation of martial law in March 1957 to meet the challenge of rebellion in the regions, the rehabilitation of areas where rebellion had erupted, the seizure of Dutch estates late in 1957 as a reprisal measure in the West Irian dispute, and the return to the 1945 Constitution and the establishment of Guided Democracy in 1959, firmly established the military in the political, economic and social affairs of the country. The army sought sufficient say in these affairs to further national development without assuming full political responsibility, and this formula, devised by Nasution, became known as the 'middle way', and was formally ratified by Congress in 1960. 'What only remained,' Nasution added, 'was how the Congress decision would be carried out.'

Under Guided Democracy, Nasution claims, the army was increasingly 'pushed aside' by Sukarno and the political parties, especially the Communist Party. His own plans for the 'middle way' involving the education and organization of army personnel in non-military jobs (called *karyawan*) were frustrated by his removal from the army command in 1962. Thus, although the 'dual function' of the army as both a defence and security force as well as a social and political force was formally established its implementation was impaired by developments under Guided Democracy.

Following the October 1965 attempted *coup,* which Sundhaussen calls the 'greatest provocation the army had ever experienced', events also showed that the army lacked anything like a 'masterplan' for taking over the government. An American scholar, Roger Paget, who arrived in Indonesia just before the *coup* and remained until early 1967, distinguishes several phases through which military-civilian relations passed before the army 'fell into the habit of governing'. From October 1965 until March 1966 when Sukarno signed the 'March 11 Order' giving General Suharto important emergency powers for maintaining law and order, his civilian support remained in the background. At this point, the 'triumvirate' of

Suharto and two civilians, the Sultan of Jogjakarta Hamengku Buwono and Adam Malik, emerged, which helped mask the military aspect of the regime. Both the Sultan and Malik were highly respected national figures, who had played prominent roles in the struggle for independence and held important government positions. However, gradually events forced Suharto into a much more prominent role within the triumvirate, and, increasingly, says Paget, a commitment to Suharto's leadership was 'not only a commitment to help defeat the Communist Party, joust with Sukarno and remake cabinets; it was also an acceptance of membership in a government where the military were clearly the senior partners'. Even so, Paget argues that army dominance flowed from the failure of civilians to rise to the occasion in the crisis situation, and a greater willingness on the part of the army to assume responsibility for the day to day demands of government.

However, army hesitation in assuming power probably stemmed partly from disunity – and a consequent inability to act decisively – as well as from lack of political aspiration. The two issues are closely related. From the outset, the officer corps was split on the general question of military involvement in the political sphere. Officers least reluctant to become directly involved were gradually eliminated from the corps through leading or joining various rebellions in the late forties and fifties. And with the emergence of Nasution's 'middle-way', differences remained. For instance, Nasution conceived an army capable of pursuing policies distinct from those of the President. In contrast, Javanese officers tended to be more fully committed to Sukarno's leadership. During 1964 and early 1965, however, the course of Sukarno's policies caused even Javanese officers, including Suharto and others to swing back more to the viewpoint of Nasution. Even so, a vast reservoir of sympathy for Sukarno within the army and among the other armed services remained following the attempted *coup*, and contributed towards the protracted struggle between Sukarno and Suharto that was finally resolved in the latter's favour in February and March 1967.

Immediately following the *coup*, Sukarno tried to assume direct command of the army, naming a comparatively weak officer, Major General Pranoto Reksosamudro, as 'caretaker' army commander, responsible for the day to day tasks. But Suharto, with the support of many senior officers, blocked this move, and temporarily assumed the army command himself. In effect, this meant the army leadership had successfully weathered the immediate challenge to its autonomy that the *coup* posed.

From this point, the army sought to press its advantage and capitalize on suspicions of Communist Party involvement in the attempted *coup*. With the bodies of the murdered generals, and the death of Nasution's daughter (who was shot during Nasution's dramatic escape from the kidnappers), the army was able to capture public sympathy, and swing the balance of power decisively in its favour for the first time for many years. However, while Suharto had little difficulty winning support within the officers corps for the crackdown on the Communist Party, the future position of Sukarno was quite a different matter. The majority of ethnic Javanese officers still harboured a strong emotional commitment to him as 'Father President', and were reluctant to discredit him. And among the other armed services, Sukarno's support was even stronger.

Even Suharto shared the dilemma of his fellow Javanese officers. Profoundly influenced by his Javanese heritage, he was a man of strongly traditional, religious-mystical persuasions. Born on 8 June 1921 in Godean, a Central Javanese village, a few miles west of Jogjakarta, his father was a minor village official charged with distributing irrigation water to the paddy fields. The young Suharto led a disturbed early life, seeing little of his parents after the first few years, and living mainly with various relatives. But raised amid the cradle of the great Hindu-Javanese dynasties, he was nourished on the way of life that the peoples of the region have safeguarded for centuries. And as a Javanese, he had welcomed Sukarno's efforts to revive the glory of their distant past, and the political outlook, values and attitudes that that past encompassed.

Suharto was also deeply committed to the army. After a brief flirtation with a career in banking, he had joined the Dutch colonial army (KNIL) as a nineteen year-old raw recruit. He apparently liked the life, did well, and rose quickly to the rank of sergeant. During the Japanese occupation, he continued his army career in the Japanese organized military forces, and with the proclamation of independence was among the first to join the Republic's fledgling forces. As a result, his personal experience spanned the army's entire short, turbulent history. He was part of its confused birth, its faltering growth, and its struggle for an identity and existence amid the turmoil of post-independence politics. He was early drawn into peripheral involvement in the political intrigue that engulfed the Republic during the armed struggle against the Dutch. He was personally involved in suppressing armed uprisings during the fifties. He had led field forces seeking the return of West Irian from the Dutch during the early sixties, and, at the time of the *coup* was commander of the army's Strategic Reserve (KOSTRAD), which was responsible for all army troops involved in the 'Crush Malaysia' campaign.

Dislodging Sukarno from the presidency involved a fundamental conflict of loyalties for Suharto and other tradition-oriented Javanese officers. Their standards of behaviour were quite strongly influenced by the code of the *satria* – the knights of the ancient Javanese realms. 'Let my neck be cut, let my hands be tied,' ran one of the pledges these warrior-administrators of old allegedly affirmed, 'I remain loyal to *guru* (spiritual adviser) and *ratu* (king).' Now, *guru* and king were in conflict. For while Sukarno was calling for calm, and no action against the Communist Party, the army was determined to bring about the total elimination of communism from Indonesia. And while Sukarno was insistent that nothing should change, that confrontation against Malaysia and the struggle for a 'new world' should continue, the army leadership wanted urgent action to begin restoring the country's run down economy. Nor was the conflict simply a question of the hold the past may have exerted on Suharto and other officers, but also their awareness of how events might be construed among millions of simple Javanese peasants. If to them Sukarno was a 'god-king', then Suharto was most probably a *satria*, and a usurper of the throne.

Frequently during the post-*coup* period, the overtones of the epic struggle of the heroes of Javanese mythology were injected into the confrontation between Sukarno and the army leaders. Suharto was personally linked with several figures – Wrekudara, Parikesit and Semar. Wrekudara, the father of Gatutkatja (a favourite of Sukarno's and his model for the new Indonesian man), is the most feared among the warriors. He scorns pomp, finery and display, bows before no man, and is merciless with his enemies. But his unswerving honesty, loyalty, courage and military skills place him among the most admired traditional heroes. Parikesit, a grandson of Ardjuna (a famous warrior with whom Sukarno was at times likened), is another *satria* who became ruler of a new kingdom after a series of bloody battles recounted in the Indonesian version of the Mahabharata. And Semar – one of the most popular and famous figures of Indonesian folklore – conveys among the Javanese even greater overtones of invincible authority. A grotesque figure, Semar is at once a clown, a man of the people, and a real force among the gods. He can flout the code of the *satria*, and seems bound by few conventions. At times, even the most powerful gods, including the Lord Shiva himself, must submit to him. And, in a sense, Suharto even upstaged Semar with his title 'Supersemar' – an acronym cleverly derived from the Indonesian for the 'March 11 Order' which he won from Sukarno during the tense days of March 1966.

Suharto also carefully avoided giving the impression

he sought to depose the 'king'. 'Return, my children, to the revolution of the people under the leadership of Bung Karno (Sukarno),' he told units of the Central Javanese Diponegoro division which were involved in the *coup* attempt. Late in 1965, he again stressed: 'As Commander of the Army, I shall never deviate from the policy and orders of the President of the Republic of Indonesia . . .' And although he was manoeuvring to isolate Sukarno from radical left-wing and communist support, Suharto was not then attempting to remove him from the presidency. Indeed, from his first public disagreement with Sukarno immediately following the *coup* over the murder of the army generals (which Sukarno wanted played down) until the dying hours of the secret debates on his future during the March 1967 session of Congress, Suharto fought for the retention of Sukarno as President, though with markedly reduced powers.

Just what powers he could have retained were clearly dependent on the degree of 'correction' Sukarno would accept. Nor was the dilemma in which Suharto found himself as a Javanese the only reason for wanting to maintain Sukarno as Head of State. More especially was the deep belief that Sukarno was still essential as a unifying symbol for the Republic, if widespread divisions and bloodshed were to be avoided. Probably also, he may have shared the widely held view that Sukarno had become a captive of his communist and left-wing supporters. Freed from their Machiavellian influence, he would again pursue a less isolated position in world affairs, and give more attention to domestic economic problems.

Events, however, generally forced Suharto's hand. Elements among both the military and the civilians were determined that Sukarno must be removed from power – though they did not usually talk openly of toppling him, but rather of giving him 'guidance'. Their attack was spearheaded through the 'action fronts' that quickly emerged in the wake of the *coup*, such as the university students' group, KAMI, and another formed among high-school children, KAPPI. These groups were frank, noisy and defiant, attacking especially the Communist Party, the cabinet, and the high cost of living. Sukarno was just as determined that he should remain master of the situation, and was desperately organizing his own support behind the scenes. As tensions rose sharply in February 1966, with clashes between opposing forces becoming more frequent, Sukarno boldly announced a new cabinet (excluding Nasution as Minister of the Armed Forces), ineffectively banned KAMI, and feverishly tried to rally support among political leaders and loyal military officers.

By March 1966, the army was playing a more open role. On two separate occasions that month, the élite troops of the army's Paracommando Corps (RPKAD) led by Colonel (later Brigadier General) Sarwo Edhie confronted the pro-Sukarno troops of the palace guards in manoeuvres that set the stage for significant formal shifts in the balance of power. On 11 March, as Sarwo Edhie's troops surrounded the palace, however, they wore no identifying insignia. On learning of their approach, Sukarno quickly fled by helicopter to his palace at Bogor, some forty miles south of the capital. It was there, later the same day, when confronted by three army generals, that he signed the 'March 11 Order' which conferred wide powers on Suharto for preserving law and order and 'safeguarding the President'. Soon, Sarwo Edhie's troops were used again to help 'flush out' a number of cabinet ministers who had sought sanctuary in the palace grounds after Suharto had issued orders for their arrest.

Suharto has always been concerned that these events should not be construed as a *coup* against Sukarno. As a result, much mystery surrounds the negotiations the three generals [late Lieutenant General Basuki Rachmat, Major General A. M. Jusuf and Major (later Lieutenant General Amir Machmud)] held with the President in Bogor. After talks lasting several hours, Sukarno signed the 'March 11 Order', although when, or by whom, the document was drafted has never been disclosed.

One of the most colourful and least likely accounts of the 'confrontation' was later provided by General Machmud. 'We were just engaged in little more than "small talk", and certainly nothing more concrete,' he told a meeting of political leaders, 'when I casually asked: "*Bapak*" (Father), these times are so difficult, and you are so much over-burdened already – why not let us handle the job?' 'Are you able to do it?', Sukarno allegedly asked. 'Yes', Machmud replied. 'All right' said Sukarno, 'you write out a draft for an order to that effect, and I'll sign it.' Sukarno's third wife, Madame Hartini, is even supposed to have prompted: 'Indeed, *Bapak* is very tired nowadays. Why not let them do the job?'

Contradicting this version, another of the generals told an American journalist, John Hughes, that the 'March 11 Order' was drafted on the way to Bogor, and that Sukarno had agreed to sign it only after lengthy, and at times, angry discussion. A third, and perhaps the most likely, possibility is that the document was drafted in Jakarta by army leaders (or at least its contents had been agreed upon) before Suharto sent the generals on their Bogor mission.

The fact remains, within a week, Suharto had used his new powers (ignoring protests from Sukarno that he was exceeding his authority) to ban the Communist Party and arrest some of the key members in Sukarno's cabinet. Included among these was the brilliant, ambitious First Deputy Prime Minister and Foreign Minister, Dr Subandrio, who had come under sharp attack since the *coup*, but had been vigorously defended by Sukarno as the 'best Foreign Minister Indonesia ever had'. But Subandrio was much more than Foreign Minister. He was Sukarno's right hand man, and headed almost every powerful policy making body in the country, as well as the President's aggressive, independent intelligence body, the BPI. Of all the ministers, he appeared to have become the most hated by the army leadership. As a result, this use of the 'March 11 Order' brought about a significant formal shift in the domestic balance of power. And since the 'March 11 Order' itself was acquired through the skilful use of force, it is difficult to see how the events of March 1966 did not constitute a quite successful 'kid-gloves', or 'mini-*coup*', especially since there is at least circumstantial evidence of planning and pre-meditation.

Even so, the 'March 11 Order' only seemed to accentuate the country's divided leadership. After concerted, behind the scenes efforts to win Sukarno over from October to December 1966 (and calculated public pressure through the trials of the former director of the Bank of Indonesia, Jusuf Muda Dalam, Dr Subandrio, and the former Commander of the Air Force, Omar Dani, for their alleged involvement in the *coup*), Suharto apparently concluded that the President's remaining powers would have to be broken. His concern was especially heightened by the activities of pro-Sukarno forces in Central and East Java, and the possibility of civil war erupting in those regions.

During December 1966, army leaders are believed to have drawn up a tentative strategy for deposing Sukarno which, among other things, set the time-table for the February and March 1967 moves against him both in parliament and congress, and decided on the release of a document detailing his alleged economic, political and moral transgressions. At the same time, other public and private pressures (especially from the leadership of Congress) were continued against the President, so that on 10 January 1967, he made a brief, provocative statement, declaring that Nasution, and others, must also accept responsibility for events leading up to the *coup*.

By the early weeks of 1967, the pro- and anti- Sukarno forces had more or less crystallized. Within the armed forces, Sukarno's strongest support came from the élite navy marines (KKO), upon whom he had earlier lavished his patronage. He also found an important following among other elements of the navy and the police, including the commanders of both these services, Rear Admiral

Muljadi, and Police General Sutjipto Judodihardjo. But his hitherto strong backing within the air force had collapsed as a result of that service's involvement in the *coup*, and the purge that had followed. And within army ranks, he still commanded considerable sympathy, although commanders controlling troops were committed to Suharto. Outside Jakarta, in the provinces, Sukarno's strongest support was generally found in East and Central Java, and East Kalimantan and parts of Sumatra. In these regions, clashes had already erupted between pro- and anti- Sukarno military and civilian forces.

Increasingly during the early weeks of 1967, Suharto found himself confronted by Sukarno's supporters. During one stormy session with the commanders of the armed forces early in February 1967, he reportedly learned that navy warships in the nearby port of Tandjung Priok had trained their guns on the Defence Department buildings. Turning to the acting army commander, General Panggabean, Suharto asked in the hearing of the navy commander: 'How long would it take to take care of this matter should it become a problem?' 'About two days,' Panggabean replied. But both the navy and police commanders continued to press Suharto during the meeting. Muljadi allegedly declared: 'Harto, if Bung Karno decides to resign of his own accord, that's okay. But if he is put before the military tribunal, the navy will strike out and declare war.' Speaking emotionally, Sutjipto added: 'We are supposed to be re-establishing the law and yet things are still happening which are not according to the law. Why was that pornographic book disseminated?', he asked, referring to the document listing Sukarno's alleged political, economic and moral transgressions. 'The police still defends the status of Bung Karno. If it is instructed by Bung Karno to move, the police will move!'

By mid-February, however, Suharto had persuaded all military commanders they must support the army position, and was able to hand Sukarno an ultimatum that he transfer all power to himself as executor of the 'March 11

91

Order'. Reportedly, Sukarno made one last effort to split the armed forces' leaders, then signed the transfer of power promulgated on 20 February 1967.

As a result, the events of that wet, grey afternoon on Sunday 12 March 1967 were something of an anti-climax. The stocky, stolid military figure fidgeting in his chair under the harsh glare of powerful TV lamps as he waited to be sworn in as his country's Acting President was still something of an enigma even among his own people. He had already won a reputation for smiling a lot, but the smile, to many, seemed rather fixed and unrevealing. And in contrast to Sukarno, he seemed very much a political novice, somehow trapped in the giant labyrinth of Indonesian national affairs almost against his will.

But the swearing-in ceremony did symbolize the dramatic turn the quest for national consensus had taken in Indonesia since the attempted *coup*. With Suharto as Acting President, and Nasution occupying the chairmanship of Congress, two army officers held the Republic's highest political posts for the first time.* Among the members of Congress, the gold braid and brightly polished buttons of military uniforms were also more evident than before. And outside the Russian-built sports hall where the ceremony was held, a khaki-flecked landscape of antiaircraft artillery placements, tanks, armoured cars, and steel-helmeted combat troops, emphasized the primary source of the army's political preeminence.

As for Sukarno, whose reign of more than twenty-one years as the most eminent, if not always the most powerful, Indonesian formally ended the same day, the lonely wait for death began. After an initial public statement that he would 'for the time being' continue to treat Sukarno 'as a President without power' (since Congress had deliberately blurred over whether he had lost the title of President as well as the power), early in May 1967 Suharto eventually dispelled any last lingering doubts by stripping him of his remaining symbols of office. But the

* Nasution was elected chairman of Congress in June 1966 when the constitutional body had first met following the *coup*.

deep emotional commitment Sukarno commanded among the Indonesian people meant that only slowly and painfully could they break with the past. During 1967, for instance, while authorities in some parts of the archipelago were removing Sukarno's portraits from places of honour, several people in East Java were arrested for defying an order from local authorities that portraits *not* be removed.

*

With the overthrow of Sukarno, concern turned more towards the question of how the army would use its new powers. What would the 'middle way' of political involvement mean now that neither Sukarno nor the Communist Party could push it aside? What were its real goals and ambitions? Did it have the capability for bringing about creative change and a brighter future for the Republic? Or would it merely become a self-interested, oppressive force? And what role would civilians be allowed to play?

During the fifties, Nasution had argued that the army would neither follow the way of Western democracies and be just an instrument of civilian power, nor the way of Latin American dictatorships and assume full political control. Instead, the Indonesian army would maintain its role – begun during the struggle for independence, and continued throughout the fifties against insurrection and rebellion – as a guerrilla force concerned with the preservation of the Republic. In such a role, he had added, it is not possible to say that a 'soldier is a soldier' or that 'politics is politics' since in guerrilla warfare, the army and the people must work closely together.

As the army explains the 'middle way', therefore, it is based on experience gained during the war against the Dutch in the late forties. 'During this struggle,' Major General Mokoginta explained to me in 1969, 'normal defence tactics didn't work, so the idea of territorial warfare evolved. We didn't fix lines of defence, but circles, or areas, of defence. Within those areas, troops operated largely on an autonomous basis, and instead of engaging the enemy in fixed lines, tried to prevent the enemy from exercising effective political and administrative control. The key to this kind of warfare was the political side – working close to the people, and "selling" the Republic in the face of Dutch propaganda.'

During the early sixties, the army decided to formulate the fruits of this experience in its defence and security doctrine. Mokoginta, who played an important part in the drafting of what became called the 'Doctrine of Territorial Warfare and Territorial Management', claims that the army leadership was convinced that the country's limited economic capacity for supporting a more conventional army meant that territorial warfare would have to remain the basis of their strategy for 'many years to come'. As a result, the army continues to consider itself responsible for the security and safety of the Republic in a very broad sense. 'We consider not only external dangers that might threaten Indonesia,' Mokoginta adds, 'but also the internal dangers of subversion, of poverty, of backwardness, of ignorance. Where these dangers arise or exist, we feel the army should take a hand in combatting them.'

With such broad concerns, the Indonesian army appears to have opened the way to almost unrestricted involvement in political, economic and social affairs for many decades to come. But the American scholar, Edward Shils, who assessed the outlook of politically involved Asian armies, including the Indonesian army, concluded that their aims were moderate – the creation of a rudimentary political society and adequate machinery of government. 'Indeed,' he adds, 'they have generally sought to conduct a polity without politics and without politicians – to run the country as if it were a large army camp ... Their programme is order and progress, but usually with more stress on order than on progress.'[1] Sundhaussen also argues that the majority of officers have

1. 'The Military in the Political Development of the New States', p. 54, in J. J. Johnson (Ed.), *The Role of the Military in Underdeveloped Countries*, Princeton University Press, 1962.

'a deep, and proven, commitment to the general welfare of the nation' rather than to sectional interests. He concludes the army is 'unlikely to establish an everlasting military regime for the sake of itself' but a prerequisite for the surrender of political control will be that the civilians 'establish their capacity to provide leadership'.

In the view of the Indonesian scholar and diplomat Sudjatmoko, it would be 'wrong – and certainly premature – to think of the military as a separate, self-seeking and self-perpetuating caste, monolithically organized and impervious to popular pressures'. He agrees that the army moved into the political arena primarily as a result of the weakness of civilian politics. He also points out, that unlike the various political parties, the army's officer corps is not tied to a particular class of society with specific interests to defend. However, he warns against the possibility that the military could become entrenched in power 'almost inadvertently through a Parkinsonian expansion of their participation in the functions of government'.

But there are factors limiting the effectiveness of military force in Indonesia, and, in the long term, these may prove the best guarantee against the entrenchment of military government. They may also impose limits upon the army's capacity to achieve whatever ambitions it harbours in the non-military realm. One aspect is the problem of the army's unity and cohesion; the other concerns what Sudjatmoko calls the 'inherent limits to what coercive power can achieve in Indonesia' as a result of the country's geographic dispersion, bad communications and economic backwardness.

Both before and since the overthrow of Sukarno, the army leadership has concentrated on repairing divisions within its own ranks and between the four armed services. It purged itself of suspected communist and pro-communist members, and pressed other services into doing the same. It also erased from its defence and security doctrine, various accommodations made to Sukarno and Communist Party pressures early in 1965, and together with the other services, has produced a jointly formulated defence and security doctrine since the *coup*. In August 1967, the separate ministries of the army, navy, police and air force (established by Sukarno in 1962 largely as an aid to playing up inter-service rivalry and thereby diluting the power of the army) were abolished by a Presidential decision, which also established the broad guidelines for integrating these services under a single command. In April 1970, a joint command was established with the reorganization of the forces under six territorial commands (KOWILHAN) – three (Sumatra, Java and Sulawesi) under the army, two (Moluccas/West Irian and Nusatenggara) under the navy, and the sixth (Kalimantan) under the air force. Each command, parallelling the central command, has a joint staff made up of officers from all services except the police, which remains a separate organization.

The army retains its basic organization into two branches: the combat units, and the so-called 'Territorial Organization'. It is the latter that has the task of maintaining the country in a state of 'combat readiness' and preventing internal unrest. The archipelago is divided into seventeen Military Area Commands (KODAM) and each KODAM has similar commands at various administrative levels, down to the village where the army is represented by a non-commissioned officer. Under the joint services command, KODAM commanders have been stripped of their former non-military powers and responsibilities, and these have been delegated to the KOWILHAN commanders. As a result, regional commanders no longer have the same opportunities to establish themselves as 'war lords', as was especially the practice during the fifties.

The army leadership also tightened control over the activities of army personnel in non-military posts. Early in 1966, it formed a special command for controlling and co-ordinating their activities, while a 'Political Team' emerged in army headquarters to deal with overall policy issues and major crises. Including the army commander (who since the reorganization of the armed forces has the title of Chief of Staff of the Army), key general staff officers, certain territorial commanders, and officers holding ministerial and other key civilian posts, the 'Political Team' can probably be accurately described as a post-*coup* 'Council of Generals'. However, after Suharto handed over the army command to General Panggabean, it was not directly linked with the office of the President, and declined in importance until its virtual disbandment in 1970.

At village level, the army also extended the scope of its 'territorial management' activities begun during the early sixties as part of its 'territorial warfare' doctrine. In December 1965, Suharto ordered the formation in Central and East Java – where the Communist Party had its greatest influence – of the 'Military Area Command' (KORAMIL) at sub-district level, and the 'Village Development Non-Commissioned Officers' (BADESA) at village level. The KORAMIL is a command post, and the officer in charge can request troops from the 'Military District Command' (KODIM) for deployment in combat, security and intelligence operations. The staff includes three senior non-commissioned officers (BATI), for operations, logistics and social-political affairs. Its job includes the detection and prevention of possible trouble and conflict at village level. It keeps a close control on the movement of all people to and from the region – no villager, for example, can travel without the approval of the KORAMIL – influences the course and conduct of local affairs, and, in general, keeps a 'weather eye' open, and exerts considerable control within the community.

Although serious divisions undoubtedly remain within its ranks, the army probably entered the seventies more united and cohesive than at any time in its history. Whether it can retain this unity while continuing to bear the burden of power remains to be seen. And whether it can provide the necessary leadership and momentum for uniting and developing the Indonesian nation is also a question only the future can answer. However, one thing is certain – the army cannot hope to govern the country successfully without the widespread support and participation of the civilian leadership and the general public.

Chapter 5

The Dilemma of Civilians

In a crowded Indonesian bus one man addresses another: 'Excuse me, is your father a military man?' 'No,' he replies. 'Is your son a military man?' 'No!' 'Is your brother, uncle or nephew a military man?' 'No!' 'Then,' shouts the first angrily, 'would you stop standing on my toes!'

•

For many civilians, this anecdote aptly sums up their dilemma in confronting the emergence of military power. They know that the military cannot govern Indonesia successfully without their political support and technical skills. But they are also acutely aware that, for the most part, the senior partners in the post-*coup* military-civilian relationship will decide who (and how) among the junior partners will share power.

At first, this was not a great concern among civilians supporting the army. Immediately following the *coup,* the objectives were clear. Those unhappy with the hypocrisy, evasion and venality of Sukarno's court under Guided Democracy, the country's tragic economic decline, the growth of the Communist Party, the Republic's growing isolation in world affairs, and so on, were in little doubt where they stood. With the overthrow of Sukarno, however, the division between the 'new order' and the 'old' continued to blur, and the military's early civilian favourites – the outspoken students and radical intellectuals – found themselves increasingly isolated.

In the early post-*coup* months, the students especially were indispensable allies of the army. They brought a new dimension to the kind of power struggle that had preceded the *coup* primarily because they flouted the tacitly accepted 'rules of the game' and, at least temporarily succeeded in changing them. The students were unconcerned about preserving appearances of unity and harmony. They were rebellious and reckless. And their raucous clamour ran counter to the atmosphere of calm Sukarno sought to effect his 'political solution' (meaning a return to the pre-*coup* state of affairs). The students rejected the traditional code under which youth respected elders and obediently followed their command. As far as they were concerned, the 'Big Father' (Sukarno) no longer 'knew best'. The traditional, paternalistic basis of authority had suffered a damaging blow.

For a while, it seemed, the army hoped it could forge an impressive military-civilian alliance using the students as a rallying point for popular support. On 23 February 1966, when nervous palace guards shot a young medical student, Arif Rachman Hakim, giving the students their first martyr, their whole movement rode a tremendous wave of public support. The following month during an army 'show of strength' through the capital, student-military relations were at their peak as the students publicly hailed the military as liberators of an oppressed people. They showered flowers upon the troops, and swarmed aboard tanks and trucks as they rolled through the streets, shaking hands with smiling soldiers and slapping them on their backs. But, within a few months, the students' outspoken and 'non-Oriental' behaviour tended increasingly to become an embarrassment for Suharto as he tried to win support among the Javanese for curtailing Sukarno's position, and he began isolating them from army support, and gradually lessening their importance within the power constellation.

The triumvirate figures of the Sultan of Jogjakarta and Adam Malik were also important partners for the army in the immediate post-March 1966 period. At that stage, the army was especially anxious not to create the impression it was toppling civilian authority, as symbolized by

Sukarno, but merely attempting to prise the President loose from his left-wing and communist 'captors'. Both the Sultan and Malik symbolized the best qualities of civilian leadership in the post-independence period, since neither had become soiled by the grubby politics of the fifties and early sixties.

Sultan Hamengku Buwono is a modern-minded monarch linked with a greatly treasured past. Born in April 1912, he succeeded to the Sultanate in 1940, and it has been preserved as a specially administered territory in Central Java largely as a result of his willingness to move with the times. Although a king among his people, tracing his lineage back to the famous Hindu-Javanese dynasties, he does not cling to the past, and turned his palace kitchen into a guerrilla headquarters during the struggle against the Dutch. But he still performs his kingly role at a muted level, and his palace is a treasure house of art from the country's 'golden age'. During the early years of the Republic, the Sultan served in many cabinets, and twice held the defence portfolio. He returned to the cabinet in August 1964 as minister in charge of state finances, but by this time, under Sukarno's leadership, cabinet had lost most of its function. In March 1966, Suharto named him special minister for economy, finance and development. He was 'acting chief executive' when Suharto first travelled abroad to Japan in March 1968, and, in the Development Cabinet formed in June 1968, was retained as a senior minister responsible for co-ordinating economic, financial and industrial affairs. Deeply Javanese beneath his Western education (Leiden, Holland), the Sultan shuns public controversy, but is less tractable than is sometimes thought.

As the second civilian member of the triumvirate, Adam Malik provided a contrasting image. Born in July 1917 in Pematang Siantar (East Sumatra), he is largely self-educated, and one of his country's most famous 'angry young men'. When only twenty, he had helped found the press agency, ANTARA, which is now the nation's official news gathering machine. For a while, he was also a prominent member of an underground communist movement led by the onetime comintern agent, Tan Malaka, and he helped found the Murba party, which was based on Tan Malaka's teachings. His association with Tan Malaka landed him briefly in gaol in mid-1946, but he claims his term in the early sixties as Indonesian ambassador to the Soviet Union cured him of his communist inclinations. He was the chief Indonesian delegate in Washington during the 1962 negotiations with the Dutch for the return of West Irian. His ability was recognized in a cabinet appointment as Minister of Trade in 1963, but by late in 1964, he was among those in the government under constant attack from communist and left-wing forces.

In the post-*coup* period, Malik was a logical choice to help the army repair the international consequences of Sukarno's 'go-to-hell' policies in world affairs. He became Foreign Minister in March 1966 (following Dr Subandrio's arrest), and also was a deputy prime minister responsible for social and political affairs until the post was abolished in October 1967. His youthful zest for life and refreshing frankness made him an immediate favourite in the government among the students. He played a leading role in Sukarno's overthrow, and was among the first cabinet ministers to publicly challenge the former President's previously sacrosanct, charismatic image. Since the *coup* he has often come under sharp attack from both the civilian 'left' and the military 'right' for his handling of foreign affairs. But opponents have found that his talents and intelligence alone make his toes difficult to tread upon, let alone keep underfoot.

But not all civilians called to the service of the 'new order' found themselves able to work under the terms imposed upon them by the military leadership. Two early casualties were the former Minister of Mining, Slamet Bratanata, and Minister of Estates, P. C. Harjasudirdja. Both were engineering graduates of the Institute of Technology, Bandung. Both had served under Guided

Democracy – Bratanata in various technical posts in communications, mining and basic industries, and Harjasudirdja as a university teacher – but were not compromised as 'Sukarnoists', and were well known to the army leadership. Both were named in Suharto's first so-called AMPERA cabinet formed in July 1966, but were among four ministers dropped in a reshuffle of portfolios fifteen months later. (The other two were eased out for their 'old order' connections and outlook.) While they were given no reasons for their dismissal, both were known to have clashed with vested army interests during their comparatively short terms in office.

As ministers, Bratanata and Harjasudirdja felt army leaders were applying a double standard in their approach to governmental affairs. For instance, on the question of the misuse of state funds. Traditionally, political parties had siphoned off state money through ministries such as mining, estates, trade and finance, for their own purposes. After the *coup*, both army and non-party civilian leaders agreed this practice should end, and, in selecting civilian cabinet ministers, Suharto paid close attention to their past party connections, their attitude towards providing state funds for political parties, and their willingness to work with army men as departmental director generals within their ministries. Both Bratanata and Harjasudirdja accepted these strictures as in the interests of restoring orderly governmental administrative and financial procedures, but later found that while state funds were no longer flowing to political parties, they continued to find their way into army coffers, both in Jakarta and the regions. Their attempts to curtail these activities brought them into conflict with army authorities, and, most likely, contributed towards their dismissal.

Another early victim of this uneasy military-civilian partnership was the chairman of the university graduates' 'action front' (KASI), Adnan Bujung Nasution. A dynamic, fiery lawyer, Bujung Nasution held a government post in the Attorney General's department. A Batak from

North Sumatra, he is talented and articulate, but often anything but diplomatic in his approach. He played a prominent role in leading post-*coup* criticisms against Sukarno, and during the March 1967 session of Congress, which withdrew the former President's powers, he spoke out strongly against the conciliatory attitude of Suharto. He was also among the most vocal critics of corruption and disregard for the 'rule of law' among alleged supporters of the 'new order', and wanted a sharp line drawn between the 'new order' and the 'old' (which was what Suharto was trying to avoid in order to prevent fresh outbreaks of violence). As a reward for his outspokenness, his seat in the country's appointed parliament (and Congress) was withdrawn on the pretext that he was due for a provincial posting and, therefore, would not be able to carry out his parliamentary duties properly when no longer living in the capital. Rather than accept complete banishment, he chose to resign from the Attorney General's department, and work as a private lawyer instead.

As the line between pre- and post-*coup* Indonesian politics continued to blur, a spirited debate erupted in the press in April 1969, underlining the vulnerability of technocrats and intellectuals especially in confronting military power. The daily *Indonesia Raya,* resurrected by Mochtar Lubis after his release from house arrest following the *coup,* carried a series of articles attacking 'intellectual prostitution' under Guided Democracy, in which it named most of the prominent civilian advisers working with the Suharto government. Lubis had a long record for outspoken journalism, and it was his attacks on Sukarno that had primarily kept him under arrest most of the time since late in 1956. Like the first flicker of a forest fire, the debate had to be swiftly doused. No one knew where it might end. 'We do not know,' admitted another paper. 'We only want to know whether the writer (of the articles) . . . did not himself collaborate with the old Order . . .'

Under Guided Democracy, the dilemma of the intellectual was clear from the reply Professor Muhammad

Sadli made to the accusations brought against him in the *Indonesia Raya* articles. In the post-*coup* period, Suharto had appointed Sadli chairman of the Foreign Investment Technical Advisory Board. As such, Sadli had become a leading advocate of attracting foreign capital for developing Indonesia's natural resources. However, the public was reminded in the *Indonesia Raya* articles that when Sukarno was in power, Sadli had argued foreign capital would only 'provoke social contradictions' and would 'never stimulate the growth of a vigorous and peaceful society' as was evident from the 'puppet state of Malaysia'. Sadli replied that under Sukarno's government, he could 'either write or remain silent'. In order to help 'preserve and develop' the faculty of economics at the University of Indonesia, he had decided to work within the 'limits of possibilities'. Sadli also sought some self-justification in the fact that 'most Indonesians believe in compromise, because without compromise, our country would have long ago split into separate states'.

One who did not compromise with Sukarno, but still managed to return to prominence in post-*coup* Indonesia was the rebel economist, Dr Sumitro Djojohadikusumo – but his comeback was not without its stormy moments. Born in Central Java in 1917, Sumitro gained a Ph.D. at the Netherlands School of Economics, Rotterdam, and founded the faculty of economics at the University of Indonesia in 1951. He held several cabinet posts during the parliamentary period of government in the fifties, joined the rebellion against Sukarno late in 1957, and went into exile when the rebellion failed. He returned to Indonesia in 1967, and was appointed Minister of Trade in June 1968. It was a highly controversial appointment in view of the widespread antipathy towards all who had joined the rebellion of the late fifties, and, like his initial return to the country, was greeted with outbursts of indignation from certain sections of the press. But his qualifications were such that they overrode political considerations.

Dr Sumitro brought a new toughness to the cabinet. A slightly built, dynamic figure, he soon set an example for his staff by arriving for work at 7 a.m. and often leaving late at night. And his practical experience was quickly felt in the way he set about curtailing the activities of market manipulators and vested military interests in trade affairs. Unlike some of his civilian colleagues, he showed he was not afraid of army opposition. 'There is always opposition from someone,' he laughs. 'The army, the banks, other departments. It doesn't worry me.'

But like the other civilian members of the economic and financial team Suharto has gathered together since the *coup,* Sumitro's durability and strength is very much a consequence of the army's determination to rehabilitate and develop the country's shattered economy. The team was well established before Sumitro's return from abroad and subsequent inclusion in the cabinet. The leading figure is Professor Widjojo Nitisastro, a quietly spoken, dedicated and skilful economist. Born in East Java in September 1927, he holds a Ph.D. in economics from the University of California, Berkeley, and was dean of the faculty of economics at the University of Indonesia before becoming the chairman of an élite economic and financial advisory team Suharto formed in 1966. In addition to being a key member of a powerful economic stabilization committee which handles day to day decisions on economic issues, he is also chairman of the National Development Planning Council (BAPPENAS), which drew up the national Five-Year Development Plan begun in April 1969. Another prodigious worker, he is probably more responsible than any other single person for the shape of Indonesia's post-*coup* economic and development drive.

Other members of the team have also been closely associated with the faculty of economics at the University of Indonesia. Dr Ali Wardhana, who was born in Central Java in May 1928, gained a Ph.D. from the University of California, and was associate dean at the University of Indonesia when he joined Suharto's team, also in 1966.

He was named Minister of Finance in the Development Cabinet formed in June 1968. Another member, Dr Subroto, was also born in Central Java in September 1928, gained a post-graduate degree from McGill University (Montreal, Canada), and a Ph.D. from the University of Indonesia, where he later lectured on international economics. He holds an important position in the Ministry of Trade as director general for marketing and trade research.

There are two Sumatrans. The Chairman of the Foreign Investment Technical Advisory Board, Dr Muhammad Sadli, born in June 1922, also studied in the United States, and holds a Ph.D. degree from the University of Indonesia. The investment board he heads provides information for prospective foreign investors, and makes recommendations to the government concerning investment proposals. Dr Emil Salim was born in South Sumatra in June 1930, holds a Ph.D. in economics from the University of California, and was also lecturing at the University of Indonesia before joining the economics team in 1966. He is deputy head of the national planning body, BAPPENAS.

Only one member of the team, Frans Seda, is actively involved in party politics. He was born in October 1926 in the Flores, gained a higher degree in economics in the Netherlands, and has a background in business. He is chairman of the small, influential Indonesian Catholic Party, and was Minister of Plantations under Guided Democracy. After the *coup,* Suharto appointed him Minister of Finance, but under pressure from Muslim political interests moved him to the Ministry of Communications in 1968, placing Prof. Ali Wardhana in the sensitive Finance Ministry.

The general cohesion of the economics and financial affairs advisory team has clearly contributed towards its successful relationship with Suharto. Through a shared past and a mutual understanding of the nature of the problems confronting the country, members have been able to establish agreement on how problems should be approached. Through their backgrounds, they have also been able to minimize the political and cultural conflict their policies and presence in the administration tend to create among certain traditional and politically antagonistic sections of Indonesian society, while still retaining the confidence of Western nations who are providing financial aid for the national economic drive.

Most of the members of the team also have links with the army that pre-date the 1965 attempted *coup*. Since the late fifties, they had often lectured at the Army Staff and Command School (SESKOAD), Bandung, and joined in army seminars dealing with military involvement in political, economic and social affairs. Several also acted as advisers in the formulation of the army's ideological doctrines. As a result, they have probably developed a closer understanding of the military than most civilians. In any event, if they share the doubts of Bratanata, Harjasudirdja, and others, concerning the ability of the army to provide Indonesia with effective leadership, they are largely able to conceal their concern, to maintain outward optimism, and to move with caution and discretion in attempting to reach their objectives.

But the alliance between military power and civilian technocracy has clearly been restricted by specific political issues. The army does not want political parties siphoning off government funds for party purposes. 'I will be frank with you,' a senior army officer told me in 1969. 'If a ministerial post becomes vacant, say for example trade. We have a choice between two courses of action. We can put in a military man who lacks experience and expertise and therefore must rely more on others for this knowledge. Or else we can give the post to a political party and they may be able to find among their members some more suitably qualified person to fill the post. But this person will be under instructions from his party, and he will be expected to provide, among other things, funds for the party and positions within the ministry and its associated bodies for members of the party. What should we do? Choose the military man, or the party man?'

The army is also more confident of its own abilities in some spheres than in others. At first, Suharto had an advisory team of civilians for political matters, but disbanded this in June 1968. On the other hand, because the army leadership lacks confidence and competence in many economic and technical matters, the importance of the economics team in the administration has continued to expand.

At times, the civilian economists have born the brunt of student criticisms, and have been accused of being 'exploited' by army interests. But all affirm their belief in the military's good intentions. During an interview with Professor Widjojo in 1969, he told me: 'The army has already brought organization to government compared with Sukarno's times. Before in the Treasury, for example, no one believed in budgets, planning and so on. To get funds for a project you had to build a model, take it to Sukarno, and make whatever changes he required – then you would possibly get funds. Everything depended on Sukarno's whims. The army has changed this. And it has already shown itself better organized and more effective than civilian administrations of the past. The army at least has an organization and regulations governing procedures clearly spelled out. This is something political parties and civilians have never been able to do.'

Chapter 6

Economics *versus* Politics

The army commander I am interviewing is shrewd and tough. 'A hungry people is not as dangerous as a hungry army,' he bluntly declares. 'So in the first instance, I am more concerned with the welfare of my boys.' It is his first regional command, and he has come face to face with the major problem confronting all regional commanders – survival. The official funds he receives from Jakarta barely cover the low salaries and allowances his troops are paid. There is not even enough money for maintaining existing buildings and equipment, let alone for buying new supplies, or developing better facilities. But he is lucky. His command covers a relatively prosperous part of the archipelago. And he finds – almost to his own surprise – that he is an able businessman. 'I didn't know I had a "cold hand",' he admits with unusual candour, '. . . that this (grabbing an object on his desk) has to be turned into money . . .'

Few military commanders are quite as frank. 'I have to do everything by my own means,' he continues. 'Resources are limited if I abide by the law.' He does not want to be more explicit, but proudly mentions building more than 1,000 houses for army families during the past three years, and re-equipping his command with, among other things, about ninety second-hand Land Rovers (bought from the departing British army in Singapore), and some seventy trucks. 'But Sumitro (Minister of Trade) is squeezing us,' he adds without malice. 'It's getting more difficult to make a profit.'

He is optimistic about the future, and impatient for action. He believes the Five-Year Development Plan can be made to work, and one of his main jobs during the coming years will be ensuring that it does – at least in the region under his command. 'Our main problem is management – the man behind the gun really,' he says, using a phrase often heard in Indonesia that should not be taken in a too literal sense. 'If he is convinced as a citizen that this is his duty to his country, we will not have too much difficulty ... (but) the real difficulty is convincing people. Sometimes this takes more energy than doing the job oneself. White collar workers see things from a political and psychological viewpoint. It's not just a matter of going ahead and doing things – they start talking ... and talking ... What we want is less talking and more action. We cannot have a welfare state by sitting on our bottoms. We have to work and sweat. This is understood by my boys. They are from the villages. But now they are used to giving orders. We will have to prepare them mentally for changes.'

The 'changes' he talks about are related to the tasks the army has assumed as a social and economic force within the country. 'We have to give an example,' he explains. 'We cannot say "let's improve production", and do nothing ourselves. People see us and say the army is not so bad if they see us doing things that are productive.' Unlike many army officers, he also doesn't quibble about who really holds power in Indonesia today. 'We have to get across the vacuum – and recognize the breakdown in civil authority. My sergeants have more authority than any of the governor's functionaries. It is not the civilian district chief, or village head, but the army man who commands. We have to get back the belief in civil authority, but meanwhile we will have to carry the burden. We are better educated, have the organization, and are more disciplined. If we give an order, it goes. But if the governor gives an order, his subordinate may say "I'll do it tomorrow", and nothing gets done. But our efforts are often misunderstood ...'

*

In a quiet Jakarta suburb, the man I now face is a highly intelligent civilian. He has held high office in the Suharto administration, but has grown disillusioned with the trend of events. Since he speaks even more frankly than the army commander just quoted, he also must remain anonymous. The army, he alleges, neither has the 'ability to lead', nor knows how to 'use its power'.

'The army lacks a sense of justice,' he continues. 'Its strategy for power doesn't even allow the heads of villages to be non-military institutions. Even the Dutch honoured that tradition. But now village heads are replaced by military men, and if not replaced, then military men are on hand to usurp their authority. Also we have this so-called "territorial management". How does it work? Take the small town of Sumedang near Bandung (West Java). I remember in the times of the Dutch when one police-man would occasionally cycle out from Bandung to keep an eye on things. Now high police officials are common-place in this town – and they're not concerned about crime. Robberies go on undisturbed. All they are con-cerned about is interfering in the distribution of rice and collecting illegal taxes.'

As a civilian, he is especially perturbed about the in-roads of the military into civilian job opportunities. 'We do not mind military figures as heads of provinces, and so on, but what is happening to the people who were trained for those jobs – who have made a career in those jobs? It was not only civilians who murdered the generals at the time of the attempted *coup*. Some of the army – some of its own people – took part in those murders. Why, then, do we deserve a lower place? We are no worse than they. And they can't fall back on the argument that the military has more expertise. They also prostitute them-selves just as much, if not more, than the civilians. Too often they have a quasi-scientific approach to a problem. The real point is that the cake is too small for all and the civilians are being kicked out. The plate of rice with a small piece of fish is all there is and the military is taking it from us without any reason or logic. They accuse us of being corrupt. As time goes on, they are even more corrupt. They accuse us of being politically weak, of being too easily influenced by this issue and that issue, and so on. But are they any better? And the longer they are in power, the less and less respect we can have for them, and for what they stand for, especially because of what they stood for in the beginning in 1966.'

Referring to a joint military-civilian seminar held in Bandung, West Java, in August 1966, the speaker adds: 'We all agreed then what had to be done, and now the first to deny the execution of those ideas is the army. They are the first to betray their own ideas . . . They don't like black-and-white people. They want to compromise. But they should practise the "rule of law". They must return to the purity of their aims. We don't want to see them misusing funds that should come to us. We don't want them kicking us out of our places. We don't want to be reduced to second-rate citizens. If all we can have is stable prices, a stable economy, and so on, then we would rather be a colony again because we know the Dutch or some other country can do this better than the army. The people's logic is being insulted if a trained man who hasn't dabbled in state funds, who hasn't abused his office, and who has trained hard for that office . . . if that man is kicked out, he can't understand why. His logic is insulted.'

*

I now turn to the collective views of a group of prominent Western international businessmen. They met in Jakarta during the latter part of 1968 to appraise the 'new face' of the Indonesian nation as an investment prospect. They were mainly concerned with three general issues – the long-term prospects for economic and political stability within the country; the purchasing power of the Indonesian market; and the degree of freedom they could expect in conducting their commercial operations in an efficient and profitable manner. Their conclusions were drawn up in a lengthy, confidential report which they presented to President Suharto, and from which the following comments have been extracted.

Investors interested in exploiting natural resources such as oil, other minerals, forests and so on, were most concerned with the prospects of stability, and the freedom they could hope for in carrying out their activities. Despite the likelihood of continued unsettled conditions during the coming decade or more, they were generally optimistic that the presence of the army as a 'moderate, stabilizing force', and the continued adherence of the government to 'sound, rational rehabilitation and development policies' should ensure 'reasonable tranquility'. As they saw the situation:

The chief threat to long-term stability . . . is abuse of power by military officials and the expansion of their vested interests, particularly in the economic realm, which could give rise to resentment and rebellion should the economic situation deteriorate. But efforts being made by the Development Cabinet, under President Suharto's leadership, to root out corruption offer hope for the future and will be watched with intense interest by the international business community.[1]

Some of the major worries for these would-be investors involved management problems. Oil companies, for instance, were concerned about the way they were obliged to enter into a vaguely worded partnership with the national oil company, PERTAMINA, which stipulated, among other things, that management – although not day to day decisions – be vested with PERTAMINA. All companies were also disturbed by the thirty year limit set on investment permits. Beyond that period, relations with the government promised to be too uncertain for comfort,

1. 'Indonesia's Prospect for Attracting Foreign Investment', a confidential report dated 17 September 1968, and representing the consensus of opinion of the Business International Roundtable held in Jakarta during that month, p. 1.

they believed, especially in view of the possibility of nationalization in later years.

Problems confronting potential investors in the manufacturing sector were far more complex. Foremost, the extremely weak buying power of the Indonesian market was seen as a great deterrent when weighed against more attractive investment opportunities available elsewhere throughout the world. To this was added a seventeen-point list of difficulties would-be investors often confronted in Indonesia ranging from burdensome taxes (despite an initial tax 'holiday') to problems with petty officialdom and competition from smugglers. At the same time, the businessmen concluded:

To list all of these deterrents to new foreign investment is not to deny the magnificent start that Indonesia has made in undoing the havoc of the Old Order and opening its doors to foreign capital, technology and managerial skills. Nor is it to suggest that in their own enlightened self-interest, international manufacturing operations will not seek ways to overcome all these obstacles and put their resources to work on behalf of Indonesia. But it is strikingly apparent that there are many steps the government of Indonesia could take that would materially accelerate the inflow of foreign investment.[1]

*

By way of contrast, I now quote from a cryptic appraisal published in an influential Indonesian business journal early in 1970:

The technocrats say 'Production has gone up'. What production, and who owns it? Giant industries . . . foreign owned and joint (foreign-domestic) ventures. And the rest? The national and people's businesses? Oh, they are flat and empty. But that is not really the question. The main thing is — production has gone up. Full stop!

The technocrats say 'Per-capita income has gone up'. Whose

1. ibid., p. 5.

income? The income of the corruptors and other money kings. But that is not the question. The main thing is — per-capita income has gone up.

The technocrats say 'Exports have gone up'. If the whole of our exports were to be affected by just one exporter alone, and his exports had gone up, then it could be taken to be so. That the other exporters are stuck is not the question. The main thing is — exports have gone up.[1]

And these were listed as 'just a few examples' of the changes to the Indonesian scene since the attempted *coup*. 'For the ordinary people,' concluded the journal, 'it's only high blood pressure that can go up!'

*

Finally, here is a hard-hitting, whimsical comment on corruption in the post-*coup* government. 'Who wants to join in playing hide-and-seek?', asks the Bandung weekly as it launches into a highly imaginative account of the 'game'. The central character, Little Gito, is the country's amiable Attorney General, Major General Sugih Arto. The 'children' he is attempting to catch are all senior army officers holding prominent posts in government and state industry, whose names have often been publicly linked with allegations of corruption in Indonesia.

'Run and hide!'
'Ready?' . . . 'Not yet.'
Little Gito, who has kept his eyes tightly shut, now opens them and looks about him trying to discover the hiding places of the other kids . . . No sooner is his attention diverted when bold little Utjup dashes for base, shouting triumphantly. Gito can only shake his head and frown. One by one, the kids run and reach base safely. Only a few have not come out yet. One is the short-legged Lam-lam, who hides behind the old man in a corner of the kitchen. Even though Gito has repeatedly peeped in this direction, the old man keeps feigning ignorance.

1. *Business News*, Jakarta, 26 January 1970.

Unfortunately, Gito detects him and promptly shouts — 'I see you. Come out, Lam!' But Lam-lam, instead of coming out like a good boy, nimbly runs for base, leaving Gito far behind him. Gito stands there open-mouthed, while Lam-lam trium-phantly shouts 'Hurrah!'

Gito is very annoyed, but the others are pleased because Gito must return to base. The old man just smiles. Two other kids, Diman and Towo are almost cornered. They are both hiding behind the well in the back yard . . . The strange thing is that the old man keeps smiling. It comes to this when children no longer observe the rules of the game. The ones in hiding can shout 'Hurrah! Base!', and no matter how hard we look for them, we will never be able to shout: 'There you are — now you're in for it!' How can we, as long as the old man just smiles?[1]

*

These are just a few glimpses of the new face of the Indo-nesian nation (warts and all) that has emerged since the attempted *coup*. They find their general focus in a slogan Sukarno sarcastically drew attention to during what proved to be the last of his famous yearly 'calls' to the Indonesian people on 17 August 1966 – the 21st anniver-sary of the Indonesian Republic. 'I was recently honoured by a scrawling on the wall which read: "Political Beacon – NO! Economic Beacon – YES!" My, oh my! How im-pressive, indeed! How impressive! . . .' He wanted no changes in national policies – domestic or foreign – after the *coup*, and certainly rejected demands that Indonesia forget about its political role as a 'lighthouse' to the 'new emerging forces' (meaning mainly the new states of Asia, Africa and Latin America) and concentrate on domestic economic problems.

Under Suharto's leadership, however, since March 1966, Indonesia had already outlawed the Communist Party, placed Sukarno's Foreign Minister, Dr Subandrio, under arrest and named Adam Malik in his place, seriously

1. *Mimbar Demokrasi*, Bundung, third week of May, 1968.

damaged relations with Peking, made peace with Malaysia, indicated its desire to rejoin the United Nations, and begun wooing the West for desperately needed financial aid for rebuilding the country's run-down economy. As such, the changes represented a radical departure from the leftward course Sukarno had steered since the early sixties, and especially since late in 1964 when he moved Indonesia into close alignment with communist China.

Turning a deaf ear to Sukarno's plea, Indonesia continued upon its changed course, disengaging from many of his most cherished positions in world and domestic affairs. Internationally, it abandoned his 'global strategy' – the crusade to 'build the world anew' –, toned down the shrillness of his struggle against 'imperialism and colonialism', and generally sought a less isolated, more respected position within the community of nations. Domestically, it rejected his 1959 political manifesto, MANIPOL (the guidelines of Guided Democracy, see p. 63), and set about a more moderate, rational and pragmatic approach to government, especially in the economic sphere. To accommodate these changes, a new political vocabulary emerged. The less emotive word 'struggle' largely replaced the somewhat pretentious 'revolution' in most official usage, 'nonalignment' returned as 'confrontation' was banished, 'peaceful coexistence' won favour over 'independence at all costs', 'economic' interests gained precedence over 'political', and 'pragmatism' before 'idealism' in a comprehensive reassessment aimed at promoting political and economic stability rather than 'controlled conflict' and turmoil.

Shrewdly reappraising the rapidly changing world scene, the new administration adopted a foreign policy aimed at maximizing foreign economic assistance without seriously jeopardizing external defence and security. It concluded that a flexible, moderate 'active and independent' policy best suited these objectives. It realized that close alignment with the United States (even if domestically possible) would not necessarily lead to liberal aid since the US was attempting to withdraw from foreign commitments, especially in Southeast Asia, rather than acquire new 'client states'. On the contrary, Indonesia's usefulness to the US – and hence the likelihood of sustained US economic aid – would more likely be enhanced by retaining the ability to act as an 'honest broker' between the US and its opponents, especially in Vietnam and Southeast Asia in general.

As a result, Jakarta maintained diplomatic representation in Hanoi, and actively courted an intermediary role in a Vietnam peace settlement. Similarly, it took the initiative in promoting regional co-operation by sponsoring the Association of Southeast Asian Nations (ASEAN), and during 1970, sought a prominent role in efforts to resolve the Cambodian crisis flowing from the overthrow of Prince Sihanouk as Head of State. While far from the ambitious role Sukarno sought as leader of the 'new emerging forces', the success of Indonesia's new foreign policy must be evaluated against its more limited objectives.

In terms of gaining economic support from Western nations and Japan, the Suharto administration has achieved remarkable success. Although handicapped by inherited debts totalling $2,100 million, it has maintained a rising level of new aid while renegotiating extremely favourable terms for repaying much of the old. Dealing with a consortium of nations known as the Inter-Governmental Group on Indonesia (IGGI), and including Australia, Belgium, Britain, France, West Germany, Italy, Japan, the Netherlands, and the United States, Indonesia raised about $1,500 million new aid during the five years from 1966 to 1970. Of this amount, the US and Japan each provided about one-third, while the remainder was raised among the other IGGI members. Early in 1970, six creditor states (West Germany, the US, France, Japan, Netherlands and Britain) owed more than $700 million by the former regime also agreed to the repayment of this debt over a period of thirty years ending in 2000 with

119

only light instalments during the first eight years, and no interest repayments until 1985 at the earliest. During negotiations with the Soviet Union later in the year, Indonesia gained similar terms for the repayment of a further $750 million in debts also accumulated during Guided Democracy. As a result, Indonesia argues that other developing countries will also benefit from the precedent now set by these negotiations for future economic aid from advanced states.

Likewise, the post-*coup* administration has gained encouraging results in attracting foreign investment. Early in 1970, Suharto announced that new investment agreed upon since the Indonesian parliament approved a foreign investment bill late in 1966 totalled more than $1,000 million. However, a large part of this amount will only be spent over a five to ten year period, and about ten per cent will probably not be realized at all for a variety of reasons. While mining – and especially oil exploration – has attracted some of the keenest foreign interest, forestry exploitation and light industries have also gained attention. By 1970, more than forty foreign companies were either hunting for new oil deposits, or helping exploit known fields. A major copper mining project involving an investment of $110 million in the mountainous wilds of West Irian is also well on the way to achieving a projected output of about 250,000 tons of copper concentrates a year by 1974. About half of more than 100 industrial projects involving a projected capital outlay of about $175 million had completed their initial plans by the end of 1970, and were involved mainly in producing construction materials and foodstuffs.

*

But what do these results mean to the country and its people? 'In which direction is our economy moving?', Suharto asked during a review of progress in August 1970. 'We must know and be convinced whether we have stagnated, regressed, or progressed, compared with four years 'ago.' He began by reminding the Indonesian people of the 'ruined economy' his administration inherited:

State finances were completely chaotic. The deficit in the state budget was extremely large and was the source of a very dangerous inflation. The state organized and controlled all economic sectors, but without direction. Bureaucracy affected every economic activity — even the smallest. Roads were in disrepair, air and sea communications were disorganized, drinking-water supplies were irregular and electricity was rationed. People had to queue for rice, kerosene, sugar, and so on. Motor cars had to queue for petrol. People in the capital and other big cities in the provinces had to stand for hours in the blazing heat before they could step into a bus or 'opelet' (small bus). People had lost faith in the rupiah (Indonesian currency), hoarding and speculation in basic commodities and raw materials were common practices, and prices jumped from day to day. Foreign loans were used for prestige projects and other projects were not based on thorough technical planning and research, thus involving waste and failing to promote development. That was the grim situation we inherited . . . [1]

Suharto then turned to what he claimed were his administration's achievements. It had curbed 'monstrous inflation' (down from 650 per cent a year in 1966 to a comparatively stabilized situation by 1969), restored order to the state finances and monetary affairs, and freed the business community from the 'improper system of "allocations"' (of import-export and other licences) and the paralysing web of regulations' that had previously stifled its activities. It had also stabilized prices of food and clothing and foreign exchange rates, ensured adequate supplies of essential materials for increasing domestic production, especially of food and clothing, improved roads, irrigation works, and so on, and improved the institutions dealing

1. 'Address of State delivered by the President of the Republic of Indonesia, before the House of Representatives on the eve of the 25th Independence Day, on 16 August 1970', Department of Information, Jakarta, p. 26.

with trade, banking and taxation. As a result, Suharto claimed, the 'condition of our economy is now better', and he added:

All of you have experienced that food and clothing are in sufficient supply and at stable prices; we do not have to queue for rice, petroleum, sugar or salt; the prices do not jump any more; communications within the city, inter-city, or inter-island are smoother, by land, sea or air. Not only within the cities, but also in the villages, there is activity and enthusiasm to work to improve and increase production . . . [1]

Suharto also gave a preliminary assessment of progress achieved under the Five-Year Development Plan. After a difficult first quarter (April to June 1969), he claimed the implementation was proceeding 'smoothly'. He said development investment during the 1969/1970 financial year had reached about $600 million. Exports during the same period had passed $1,000 million – nine per cent higher than the target for the first year of the plan, and not far short of the record export level of just over $1,000 in 1951. (By comparison, exports during 1963 and 1964 were running at about $650 million a year.) Imports had also increased to more than $1,000 million, but these, he said, included goods needed for raising domestic production. Rice production at 10.8 million tons was higher than the plan's first year target, and production had also risen in estates, forestry, livestock and ocean fisheries. On the other hand, production of some agricultural crops, such as cassava and maize, and of inland fisheries had declined. In the industrial sector, textile production had risen by thirty per cent, and increases were also recorded in cement, tyres, soap, coconut oil and some other commodities, with declines in the output of fertilizers and cigarettes. Mining, and especially oil, had shown good gains. Many of the increases, Suharto added, flowed from progress made in rehabilitating and developing roads, bridges, dams and

1. *ibid.*, p. 28.

irrigation works, as well as from better transport and tele-communication facilities.

*

Few Western observers familiar with the pre-*coup* Indonesian economy quibble over the significance of these achievements. The situation the administration inherited in 1966 was every bit as bad as, and probably worse than, Suharto depicted in the passage quoted above. The improvements he claimed were also probably a reasonable assessment of progress made during the first four years of his administration – progress some Western economists find quite exciting. Doubts could easily be raised about the likely permanence of some of the gains, but generally the results indicated an encouraging trend. Whatever its shortcomings, the administration was at least treating economic problems seriously, and with some success – something that had hardly ever happened, if at all, during the pre-*coup* era of Sukarno's 'guided economy' and 'lighthouse' political policies.

Yet during the late sixties and early seventies, politically vocal Indonesians (including those who helped overthrow Sukarno) remained largely unimpressed by the Suharto 'face-lift' – a fact he acknowledged in his progress report. Wryly, however, he claimed some headway in meeting their dissatisfactions. At the beginning of 1966, he said, three demands were heard: the dissolution of the Communist Party, the lowering of prices, and the purge of the Sukarno cabinet. By early in 1968, these demands had changed to two: the lowering of rice prices and the eradication of corruption. And from early in 1970, he noted, they had been narrowed to a solitary cry – step up the eradication of corruption.

Even so, much more than corruption underlies the cry of demonstrators as they spill out into the streets of Jakarta with their handbills, paint pots and penchant for embarrassing questions. We want to know . . . , they demand . . . Why a Suharto aide (named) keeps state funds in a foreign bank account under an assumed name . . . Why the state oil monopoly, PERTAMINA, ordered $25 million worth of tankers through a broker and not directly from a ship-building company . . . Why such-and-such a scandal involving $711,000 of state funds had not been prosecuted by the Attorney General . . . Why the state rice buying agency, BULOG, can run up an overdraft with Bank Indonesia of nearly $200 million . . . How a certain minister or military commander, considering his low salary, can live such a life of luxury . . .

Partly the public clamour arises from the fact that for many urban dwellers life is generally just as tough — or even tougher — than during Sukarno's time. It may be true that prices are more stable, food and clothing are in good supply, communications are better, and even real wages have risen somewhat. But all this often provides cold comfort in contrast with the 'feather-bedding' Sukarno provided city dwellers at the cost of the country's long-term interests.

Under Guided Democracy, the expropriation of foreign property, the weakening of important entrepreneurial groups associated with the outlawed Islamic party Masjumi, and the curtailment of the private sector of the economy, all led to a significant redistribution of wealth among the politically more prominent, essentially urban elements of society (including the military, the bureaucracy, and pro-government political and business interests), but seriously affected production and economic growth. Urban communities also benefited from other government policies, such as the heavily subsidized essential services (water and electricity rates were often so low they were not worth collecting), the government purchase of farm produce at unrealistically low prices, the expansion of the bureaucracy and state enterprises, and the plethora of controls and regulations that widened the scope for supplementing incomes through graft and corruption. Prestige building programmes, too, provided work for many of the otherwise unemployed. And even the inflationary conditions offered welcome opportunities for both large scale speculators and profiteers, as well as for countless petty traders.

Post-*coup* economic reforms reversed most of the material ways Sukarno helped underpin his popularity among the politically vocal urban communities. The abolition of subsidies for public utilities and other state enterprises, as well as the periodic rises in petrol and kerosene prices, brought about quite substantial increases in the cost of living for many city dwellers, and a direct loss in income for some. The need to reduce government spending and increase government revenues caused a further decline in jobs, such as the prestige projects had earlier provided, and an intensification of efforts to collect taxes and other government service charges. With the jettisoning of cumbersome controls and regulations in some ministries, such as trade, opportunities among petty bureaucrats for supplementing incomes also were affected. Inefficient government backed business suffered through the withdrawal of government support, tighter credit, and increased competition from private interests. In brief, those often hardest hit by the post-*coup* stress on pragmatic economic issues were the white collar workers who were among the main beneficiaries of Sukarno's pre-*coup* emphasis on the political and ideological which largely led to the economic mess the Suharto administration inherited.

A further cause for civilian unrest stems from the fact that Indonesia has more military forces and civil servants than the country can afford. Official figures dealing with this question are invariably vague and contradictory, but it is extremely doubtful whether even the government can estimate the real cost of this burden. Some estimates put about 3,000,000 people (including about 500,000 in the armed forces) on various central and regional government and semi-government payrolls of one kind or another. Again, figures may not be very reliable, but those presented by the Wilopo commission inquiring into corruption (see p. 127), indicate that the government paid out nearly $1,000 million in salaries to civil servants alone during 1970 (roughly equivalent to the country's total export earnings), and this sum was probably only enough to meet about one-third of the cost of living for these people and their dependents. Similarly, the official budget for the military probably only meets about one-third of the real cost of maintaining the country's armed forces. Under Guided Democracy, Sukarno postponed dealing with this problem at the high cost of depleting the country's existing economic resources, and through neglecting to spend money on urgently needed new development. And under the post-*coup* administration, which has given priority to these matters, it is not so surprising that civilians living in the cities are feeling the 'squeeze' more than their military colleagues, while the latter hold the upper hand.

Public unrest also reflects the impossibility of achieving spectacular results in the economic sphere. Suharto has often warned the Indonesian people, as he did at the end of 1966, that he would not 'promise there will be all-out changes overnight – that the living conditions of the people will all of a sudden change to the better'. Nonetheless, only if the general public can be persuaded they are benefiting from the administration's efforts – especially when those entail repeated calls for austerities – will there be much hope of overcoming the widespread scepticism and malaise that has grown among the people as a result of more than two decades of unfulfilled hopes and broken government promises. Yet able administrators, such as the Minister of Trade, Dr Sumitro Djojohadikusumo, believe that it might be nearly twenty-five years before much concrete progress can be made. Few responsible officials, in fact, expect much noticeable change within the coming decade, such are the overwhelming economic problems the country confronts, even if political and economic stability can be maintained.

Nor is this difficult to understand. Under the Five-Year Development Plan from 1969 to 1974, for instance, the projected expenditure on development totals about $3,500 million. The plan is oriented towards improving agricultural production. If completely successful, planners hope for a 47 per cent increase in rice production (eliminating the need for rice imports), and production increases ranging from 25 per cent to more than 38 per cent for corn, sugar, vegetables, fruits and fish. Meat production is expected to climb by more than 67 per cent, milk by nearly 150 per cent, and egg production by more than 220 per cent. Likewise big gains are sought in the output of palm oil, copra, cacao and other agricultural export crops. All this is supposed to add up to a real increase in farmers' incomes, but increased production does not always mean increased profits for farmers.

In its desire to provide cheap food for politically vocal urban communities, the government often runs counter to the farmers' interests, destroying their incentive to even try to produce more. And if the farmers are not given adequate incentives, then the agricultural targets set under the plan are unlikely to be reached even if the administration succeeds in finding the necessary funds for the plan's implementation. On the other hand, if the gains accruing from increased farm output do find their way into farmers' pockets, city dwellers are unlikely to find their life dramatically improved during the coming decade. For even if the plan is 100 per cent successful in every sector – rural, mining and manufacturing – real national wealth is not expected to rise by more than a yearly average of about five per cent. And with population increasing by about $2\frac{1}{2}$ per cent every year, the impact of this gain is immediately halved.

Against this background, corruption and 'conspicuous consumption' among the wealthy few (both military and civilian) pose a major threat to the possible success of the post-*coup* administration. Early in 1970, under considerable pressure from public demonstrations, Suharto appointed a four-man commission to probe the problem. They were a former Prime Minister Wilopo, and three other national figures who had held cabinet rank during the early fifties – I. J. Kasimo, Anwar Tjokroaminoto and Professor H. Johannes. After inquiries lasting five months. they claimed to have gained a 'clear picture of our common problem', reporting, among other things, that the 'government has to overcome a great deal more in its efforts to eradicate corruption, and that results of its attempts so far are inadequate compared with the vast scope of the problem'.

According to the Wilopo commission, corruption in Indonesia was 'growing rampant' and had 'emerged in new forms'. 'Especially in the last three to four years,' the report continued, 'there have been extremely luxurious ways of life giving rise to questions about the sources of this wealth.' Pointing to new opportunities for corruption arising from foreign credits, foreign capital, the liberalization of foreign exchange, the 'oil boom', 'lumber boom', and the 'boom in government purchases for projects', the commission concluded that 'there is real need for a hard policy to prevent corruption and to eliminate or reduce its causes.' Added the report:

It is generally said that the major reason is moral decline. People no longer know what is corruption and what is not. In daily conversation, people admire cunningness in acts of corruption by forging of valuable documents, briberies, elimination of proof, particularly on the part of powerful and moneyed individuals. No wonder prosecutors are heard to say: 'Yes, I know of those practices, but how can they be proved.' A minister told a member of the commission: 'If I can eradicate corruption, I'll do it, but morale has gravely deteriorated.' These voices obviously encourage the corruptors . . . [1]

But even curbing, let alone eradicating, corruption poses a herculean task in Indonesia. For one thing, what the West may regard as corruption is often seen as the rewards of achieving high office in many Asian countries.

1. *Sinar Harapan*, Jakarta, 24 July 1970.

Further, the inability of the government to pay a living wage to its employees means that making up the difference through exploiting one's position is generally not regarded as corruption. And this has led to a blurring of the boundaries between what is right and wrong, and how far it is permissible to go. Traditional customs and attitudes also impose further pressures on prominent officials to profit from their positions for personal gain and the vested interests that have often helped them reach a position of power. Those at the top are expected to protect the interests of their families and friends, their military units, their political party, their department, or whatever it might be. Despite protestations to the contrary, the overall national interests invariably come a poor second best. Also the higher a person rises, the more appearances he is expected to maintain – a more luxurious house, bigger limousine, wider circle of dependents, and so on. As a result, corruption and the sources of power are intimately intertwined.

Outbursts against corruption by the press and public in Indonesia are also not always inspired by the purest of motives. Often competing vested interests agitate against certain officials mainly in the hopes that their own candidates may succeed to their lucrative positions. Thus removing an official – especially if he is otherwise capable and experienced in the post – may only worsen the overall situation. Further, corruption is highly contagious. New procedures and apparatuses set up to fight corruption are often themselves quickly corrupted. Likewise leaders of anti-corruption campaigns have also themselves sometimes proved unable to withstand corruption's temptations as they arise.

It is not yet clear whether Suharto can cope with the problem of corruption, or to what extent he is even committed to trying. He has stressed the importance of eliminating the causes of corruption rather than concentrating on dramatic repressive measures which could only achieve transitory results. He also warns against overreacting to 'eye-catching items about corruption' (under Sukarno these items were usually not even allowed to be published). '... don't let this make us lose confidence in ourselves; do not let such news items on corruption make us doubt the fact that development has started to be carried out and that it has already achieved many results,' he argues. 'Let us not mix assumptions with fact.'

Even so, unless the country's top leadership can set a better example, it is difficult to see how the new face of the Indonesian nation can help but be obscured by the blemishes of corruption and other excesses. The early stress on austerity that followed immediately after the *coup* – and served the political purpose of contrasting the economic concern of the 'new order' with the profligacy of the 'old' – quickly became submerged in a deluge of dollars pouring in from abroad. Half-hearted attempts to stem the flow of luxury cars into the country were soon abandoned (mainly because they did not work). And with a few notable exceptions, especially among the civilian economic experts, not many close to the seat of power do not today live in far finer houses, and in a grander style, than was the case before the attempted *coup*. Yet these are the people who must call upon the majority of the population to 'tighten their belts' and have patience since living conditions cannot be improved overnight.

If the leadership cannot convince the general public that it also shares the 'sufferings of the people' – and so far it has failed on this count – the prospects for continued political and economic stability must grow increasingly remote. Already, criticisms of government foreign and economic policies are widespread. Many are far from happy with policies that make Indonesia appear a 'nation of beggars', and as though the country is 'up for sale' to the highest foreign bidder. Critics argue the government has moved too close to the West, and at high cost to the country's political and economic independence. They profess concern that the Indonesian 'face-lift' no longer reflects a vigorous anti-colonialist and anti-imperialist outlook. They even fear that their economy has become allied to, and dependent upon, imperialist economic power. They also hunger for the world prominence and notoriety Indonesia achieved under Sukarno's foreign policy. Thus as long as the present economic approach to nation-building can only be seen to be benefiting a few, and those few continue to flout their wealth, the 'Political Beacon' Sukarno favoured will most probably regain its allure.

Chapter 7

Invisible Government

The contrast between the policies and strategy of pre- and post-*coup* Indonesia should already be clear. But does the style and pattern of government really differ from the old?

*

The voice answering the phone is clipped and matter of fact. 'Senopati street', he says, then awaits your inquiry. The phone has rung in a three-storey building most people hardly notice as they swing past a busy traffic round-about on the outskirts of Jakarta's residential satellite town of Kebayoran. At first glance, the building could be (and once was) a block of well-appointed flats. Balconies and the backs of air-conditioners jut from its whitewashed windowed walls. Then the flat-topped guard house and steel-helmeted guards partly hidden by garden shrubbery, the assorted military registration plates on the vehicles parked within the ground, and the spidery antennae of a complex communications network, come into view. For 'Senopati street' is the headquarters of BAKIN – the body formed following the 1965 attempted *coup* to replace the BPI (Central Intelligence Body) that had earlier become a legendary force under the leadership of the former Foreign Minister, Dr Subandrio. And like the BPI, BAKIN has come to exert a growing indirect influence on the everyday lives of Indonesians largely through acting as the 'eyes and ears' of the administration. It also functions as a 'think tank', evaluating problems, crises and questions of policy for the president and cabinet. At times, BAKIN may even play a more active intelligence role, but this is normally the function of OPSUS.

OPSUS is the Indonesian acronym for 'Special Operations'. Its boss, Brigadier General Ali Murtopo, is a member of the élite corps of special assistants to the president, or ASPRI, as they are generally known within the country. Ali Murtopo is a genial Javanese whose links with Suharto date back to the early fifties. He is often jokingly referred to among Indonesians as 'the man from Raden Saleh street' rather than directly by name. Although he has offices in BAKIN, Raden Saleh street is where he prefers to work. It is more approachable for his part-time informants and agents, and closer to the president's personal residence in Tjendana street. A highly skilled and experienced intelligence officer, Ali Murtopo has continuously engaged in 'silent operations' for Suharto, both domestically and abroad, since even before the attempted *coup*.

Born in Blora, Central Java, in 1924, Ali Murtopo was educated in Central and West Java, and fought with the Diponegoro (Central Java) division during the independence struggle against the Dutch. He became a company commander in the Diponegoro's élite 'Raiders' when the paracommando unit was formed in 1952, and still proudly wears his 'green beret'. It was also about then that his close association with Suharto began. Later, in 1958, he was briefly on Suharto's staff when Suharto commanded the Diponegoro. He joined him in Jakarta in 1960 when Suharto was a deputy chief of staff in army headquarters, and, after intelligence and liaison work in West Irian, again in 1963 when Suharto became commander of the army's Strategic Reserve (KOSTRAD). In this position, he also developed KOSTRAD's OPSUS which played a major behind the scenes role in settling the Malaysian dispute.

In the post-*coup* period, Ali Murtopo emerged as one of the military's liveliest intellects and a leading 'trouble shooter' for the president. In the wide range of difficult assignments he has handled, he has frequently shown an ability to break through 'bottle-necks' and get results where others have failed. Take, for instance, his role in the 'Act of Free Choice' conducted in West Irian under the supervision of the United Nations in 1969. His main task was to ensure the Irianese voted to remain within the Republic. As part of this effort, his men mounted a massive logistics operation in the territory (compared with past neglect during the years since 1963 when Jakarta first assumed administrative control over the region) to win over a rather disgruntled and disillusioned people. Shop shelves, long since bare of all but a few unsaleable odds-and-ends, suddenly were crammed with tinned food-stuffs, toilet articles, household goods, and, especially, the Irianese people's favourite brand of Dutch beer. At times, newspaper correspondents trying to contend with the territory's fickle and infrequent air services found that OPSUS had almost every available plane on charter, some of which were flying in gifts, including pigs, for influential tribal chiefs in the remote highland regions.

In domestic political affairs, the measure of Ali Murtopo's success can often be gauged by the level of public outcry against him. For instance, when the Nationalist Party (PNI), which is probably the largest of the country's nine political parties, elected a Central Javanese, Hadisubeno Sosrowerdojo, as its national chairman in April 1970, the students' paper, *Harian KAMI*, alleged he was successful 'because of OPSUS'. According to the students, Ali Murtopo 'co-ordinated the interference' in PNI affairs from a 'command post' nearby the site where the elections were held. His men were also supposed to have met and lavishly entertained many of the delegates as they arrived for the meeting, and generally spread the word that the party's future good fortunes depended very much on Hadisubeno gaining control of its executive body.

Inevitably, this kind of political pressure evokes comparisons with the methods of Guided Democracy. One of

Sukarno's favourite means of making his 'wishes' known was to relay them quietly by way of the commander of his élite palace guards, Brigadier General Muhammad Sabur. Although Sabur was eventually gaoled following the attempted *coup*, his memory has been perpetuated through the coining of a political term 'saburism', which is now used to describe activities such as Ali Murtopo's during the Nationalist Party elections.

Ali Murtopo is only one of several close aides on whom Suharto often relies. Among the most prominent of these is another special assistant (ASPRI), Brigadier General Sudjono Humardhani, who has also played an important behind the scenes role in the political and economic affairs of the post-*coup* administration. Born in Salatiga, Central Java, in December 1919, Sudjono chose an army career rather than join his father's business. He also served under Suharto when the latter was commander of the Diponegoro division, and after a series of financial posts with the Diponegoro, was appointed deputy comptroller of the army in Jakarta. His military education includes studies at the Fort Benjamin Harrison Finance School in the United States. In contrast to the extroverted Ali Murtopo, Sudjono usually avoids the limelight. He is also deeply influenced by traditional Javanese beliefs, and an office at his house where he receives a constant stream of political and economic leaders is dominated by a large painting of a *satria* (Javanese knight) consulting with his *guru* (spiritual adviser) before embarking on a difficult mission. 'It's up to you whether you believe in it or not,' he told me once during a meeting. 'But if a person seeks guidance from God before he acts, he will always act rightly. It is what is needed in the world today, not just in Indonesia, but in Europe, in Australia and elsewhere.'

For many Indonesians, the influence of BAKIN, the activities of OPSUS, and the power of the ASPRI, are symptoms of the shortcomings of government in Indonesia today. They see themselves as being ruled by an 'invisible government' rather than by the formal institutions of congress, parliament and an administrative apparatus controlled by a presidential cabinet. They are concerned that ASPRI appears at times to function as a 'super cabinet', and that power has become divided between the constitutional bodies and this élite group of inner presidential aides who have no constitutional standing but wield immense influence in day to day affairs. They also question the capabilities of these élite, asserting that some hold office more through accidents of history that have brought them close to the president than from proven ability.

Such accusations put only one side of a very complex problem. When Suharto came to power, he inherited a largely bankrupt, impotent system of government. One of his tasks is to establish a more workable and acceptable alternative. He has made efforts to strengthen congress and parliament, but these efforts largely ended in failure. He has also tried to improve cabinet and make the administration function more effectively and efficiently, but this is a long-term pursuit involving political, social and economic questions. And in the meantime, he must still cope with the realities of trying to rule and develop a diverse people inhabiting more than 3,000 islands throughout the archipelago. To do this, while lacking effective formal institutions of government, he is often forced to devise and exploit novel and irregular ways of securing and maintaining effective power, of formulating national policies, and of convincing a sufficient majority of people of the appropriateness of those policies and of the government's ability to carry them out.

Ali Murtopo's activities in the Nationalist Party elections mentioned above partly illustrate this point. Under Guided Democracy, the party had fallen under the control of radical elements, and, at least at national level, pursued policies generally indistinguishable from those of the Communist Party. Following the *coup*, the military brought about the overthrow of the radical leaders, restoring control to moderate, anti-communist leaders. In

Central and East Java, however, which accounts for the majority of members, these leaders met only a lukewarm and even hostile response since they generally represented the urban and West Javanese and Outer Islands' elements of the party. Concerned over the need for a closer working alliance with the party's 'grassroots' among its Central and East Javanese elements (especially with the approach of national elections, scheduled for July 1971), Suharto threw his weight behind the election of the strongly anti-communist Hadisubeno, rather than a more senior, and possibly more brilliant, contender for the office, Hardi.

But underlying the vigorous press outburst against Ali Murtopo's involvement (early in 1966 when the army forced out the radical leadership the same papers had raised no protest, but some had applauded) was a further issue of major political significance. Despite the professed ideological bases of most Indonesian political parties, factions within a particular party often find they have more in common with elements of other parties than with rivals within their own ranks. In the case of the Nationalist Party, Hardi and his supporters represented the more moderate, city-based elements of the party. As long as these elements retained a dominating position at national level within the party, the possibility of a broad civilian alliance with other like-minded parties remained, such as the alliance that had been formed between the Nationalist Party, the Masjumi and the Socialist Party (PSI) during the early fifties under parliamentary democracy. However, with the election of Hadisubeno, and the exclusion of Hardi from the executive, the position of traditional rural Javanese and 'Sukarnoist' forces within the party were greatly strengthened.

Since the *coup*, Suharto's strategy in dealing with political parties has generally aimed at preventing violent swings in political fortunes and protecting the unity of the army. He has obviously been anxious not to become a captive of any political party or alliance of civilian political forces, and has actively courted the widest political support. As a result, only after a long delay and much negotiation (in which personal aides played a major role) did he agree to the formation of a new Muslim party instead of the revival of the outlawed Masjumi, which would have caused widespread repercussions within the army and among traditional Javanese political elements. At the same time, he worked actively to strengthen the position of the Nationalist Party (after effecting a purge of its more radical and left-wing elements) partly as a counter to Muslim power in the absence of the Communist Party. And it is generally against this background that his political 'interference', and the press outcry of frustrated political forces must be viewed.

Indeed, Indonesian domestic politics is generally such a political jungle that it is difficult to see how Suharto could survive without assigning important roles to bodies like BAKIN, OPSUS and ASPRI. Partly, it is a question of needing people he can rely on and trust, whatever their personal short-comings, partly, also, the question of getting things done. Ali Murtopo, Sudjono, and other close aides that Suharto relies on are foremost people he can trust. An aide once told me, for example, that on the eve of the March 1967 session of Congress, many political figures publicly claiming to be supporting Suharto were, in fact, actively working for Sukarno's return to power.

Suharto also denies that his personal aides have any policy-making role. 'You may ask cabinet ministers,' he told protesting students in July 1970. 'They (ASPRI) attend cabinet meetings, but never make speeches. They assist the leadership in checking and rechecking information so that control will be more comprehensive. They serve as liaison men to collect views and ideas to help me in my tasks as national leader.' However, under continued pressure from student demonstrators, Suharto issued a presidential decision early in August 1970 which detailed the duties and authority of all ASPRI, specifically mentioning that they did not have any executive powers. Even so, few expected the dispute to end on that note.

*

Suharto's power is derived from two primary sources: from the office of the presidency and from the authority he still retains over the army as the Minister of the Armed Forces, and as a former commander and active officer. He has generally succeeded in consolidating his control over the army by changes made within the structure of the army and armed forces since the attempted *coup* (p. 96). As a result, compared with Sukarno, who failed to gain control over the military establishment, Suharto's position is much stronger. But Suharto lacks the charisma and popular hold Sukarno commanded among the Indonesian people. And the reality of his constitutional power and military control when put to the test is often not as formidable as appearances might suggest.

In theory, the office of the Indonesian president is an enormously powerful post. Under the 1945 constitution, the president assumes executive authority and shares legislative power with parliament. He has a say during the processing of parliamentary bills, as well as the final say. No bill can become law without his signature, and he cannot be forced to sign. He is not bound to reflect a parliamentary majority in his cabinet, and neither he, nor his cabinet ministers (who are only his assistants), are directly responsible to parliament. In fact, the president is directly responsible only to congress which is too cumbersome a body to convene often or speedily.

Congress (MPR) holds the highest authority of state. It determines the constitution, the guidelines of national policy, and appoints the president. It is formed from the membership of parliament, delegates from the regions, and representatives of workers' associations and other collective bodies. It must meet at least once every five years (the term for which the president is appointed), but during the crisis period following the 1965 attempted *coup*, congress met in mid-1966, March 1967 and again in March 1968.

Parliament (DPRGR) is the legislative body. It must approve all draft laws and regulations originating from the executive. Members also have the right to initiate laws. It controls the president indirectly through its authority over the budget, and its power to convene congress in special session if it believes the president has overstepped his mandate. But neither of these provisions has proved effective as a curb in the past.

Both the congress and parliament Suharto inherited were formed by Sukarno in 1960. Pending elections (which were never held), Sukarno named the membership of a 283 member parliament and a 616 member congress. While his appointments were widely representative, they understandably excluded his bitterest opponents, and especially the Islamic and socialist party elements which had played a major role in the 1958 rebellion. Following the *coup*, Suharto made further changes in the size and composition of both bodies, excluding especially communist and pro-communist elements, and adding 'new order' supporters.

Initially, Suharto did succeed in giving both congress and parliament new authority. They no longer appeared so obviously 'rubber stamps' for decisions made elsewhere as had been the case under Guided Democracy. But the steamroller approach he adopted in preparing for the March 1968 congress gave rise to deep concern among many civilians. The session convened mainly to extend his mandate, to approve a five-year development plan, and to postpone general elections (scheduled for 1968 by a decision of the mid-1966 congress). However, the removal of Sukarno from the presidency twelve months earlier had created an extremely fluid political situation. No longer united in common opposition to Sukarno and the Communist Party, rival factions within the 'new order', and contenders among the 'old', were again jockeying to safeguard, consolidate and extend their various interests.

Although the agenda at the 1968 congress seemed clear-cut, the precise terms of the president's renewed mandate, the question of how long elections might be delayed, and the way both of these issues might be tied to the proposed development plan, all carried significant political ramifications for various army and civilian interest groups. In addition, the agenda raised the broader and more fundamental conflicts between military and civilian authority, and concerning Islam, especially as congress was to examine basic state policy, seeking alternative guidelines to Sukarno's 1959 political manifesto (MANIPOL), and a new statute of human rights.

As a result, Suharto found agreement increasingly difficult to establish although he was under growing pressure for tangible results. During 1967, his caution and policies had led to a strong feeling that his administration lacked a sense of purpose and direction. The cost of living continued to climb (quite dramatically during late 1967 and early 1968 through a jump in the price of rice), and life for the average Indonesian had certainly not improved, and for many, had probably grown harsher. Moreover, 'new order' leaders were under attack for being just as corrupt and incompetent as the 'old', and concern was rising among civilians that the octopus-like tentacles of the military would soon occupy every comfortable and profitable nook and cranny they had previously held.

These circumstances probably left Suharto little alternative but to adopt a tougher approach. He began his search for support in the latter part of 1967 by partially conciliating Nationalist Party and Islamic political forces. He lifted restrictions at that time imposed on the Nationalist Party in Java and Sumatra, and agreed to the formation of a new Islamic party, the Indonesian Muslim Party (Parmusi, or PMI). And he appeared to give some concessions to radical army and civilian groups who were vigorously pressing for a sweeping purge of 'old order' elements in both parliament and congress, and a drastic overhaul of the whole political system, by 'redressing' parliament early in 1968. Its membership was raised from 347 to 414 members (with the military gaining 32 new seats for a total of 75, and the 'action fronts' receiving a further 20 seats), and 117 members were replaced after discussions between Suharto and the political parties and organizations they represented. But the abruptness with which he finalized these changes partly contributed towards criticisms brought against him.

Suharto eventually gained agreement in congress for his minimal demands – but not without cost. His emergency powers under the 'March 11 Order' were more specifically defined, and his image as a protagonist of democratic procedures was somewhat tarnished. The arrest and injury of students during pre-congress demonstrations, the massive deployment of military force during congress (reportedly thirty battalions), and the strong-arm tactics of his aides and 'project officers' during the session, led to a new level of disenchantment among even his most ardent civilian supporters. He was also forced to impose tighter discipline on army radicals, further weakening their civilian support and highlighting the conflict between army and civilian interests in a deeply divided country. At the same time, the chasm between the traditional Javanese and the non-Javanese Islamic belief was again underlined as attempts to draw up a basic state policy ended in deadlock, and had to be abandoned. Further, congress and parliament had lost much of their lustre as forums for expressing consensus and 'national will'. While still less obviously 'rubber stamps' than during the days of Guided Democracy, real power clearly resided outside these formal institutions as the important decisions were unmistakably being made elsewhere, so that the 'constitutional way' long stressed by the Suharto administration could not help but acquire an increasingly hollow ring.

Subsequently, Suharto regained some lost prestige through the formation of a new Development Cabinet in June 1968. By reducing military representation from nine to six (and the number of army ministers from six to four) in a twenty-three member cabinet, he revived civilian hopes that he meant what he said about wanting to return power to civilians, although key political posts (Domestic Affairs, Defence and Security, Information, Industry and Labour) remained in military hands. He also disbanded his original twelve-member 'personal staff' (SPRI), which had been much criticized for usurping cabinet's function, but kept five of the most important members in similar posts, giving several the new title of ASPRI, which continues to rankle. Nor, except in a very tentative way, had Suharto come to grips with the basic questions raised by the failure of Guided Democracy, such as who would share power with the army, and how. Instead, he appeared to be bogged down in a shoring up operation – desperately trying to dampen down the pendulum swings of post-independence politics by ensuring that the Islamic forces did not get too strong while the secular, nationalist forces remained weak; that the precocious, Western-oriented radical forces among the army, civilians and students were kept in check; and that the army remained united and firmly under his control.

In a sense, Suharto had become ensnared in a web of his own spinning. By choosing the 'constitutional way', he had become a prisoner of what one commentator has called an 'almost obsessive insistence on "consensus"'. The Australian historian, J. D. Legge, likewise noted the danger inherent in Suharto's commitment to 'restore democratic procedures' since it could result, not in the desired democratic goals, but merely in the discarding of 'rational government'[1] in favour of the 'free play of self-interested pressures'. By early in 1968, this increasingly seemed the trend. (By mid-1970, a logjam of more than 100 bills awaited 'consensus' in parliament.) And while his hands were increasingly tied at national level, his administration's 'image' continued to suffer through arbi-

1. 'General Suharto's New Order', *International Affairs*, January 1968, p. 45.

trary exercise of power at the lower levels of government, and especially in the regions.

But Suharto probably had little real choice. A possible alternative course – a radical overhaul of government backed by military power – could scarcely have appeared attractive, if at all possible. After the turbulence of Guided Democracy, the army leadership was divided, and many of its officers seemed confused and uncertain. The country's run-down economy, bad communications and geographic dispersion could not help but blunt, and even thwart, the effectiveness of military power for enforcing reforms, even if the armed forces were united. The archipelago also lacked a responsive, disciplined administration capable of implementing unpopular orders. Both military and civilian officials – especially in the regions – had long since grown accustomed to 'reinterpreting' central government directives to suit their own purposes. To these considerations must also be added the problem that Indonesia's diversity presents.

The problem of the bureaucracy has already been mentioned (p. 125). It is over-swollen, underpaid, and riddled with corruption and the consequences of political nepotism and intrigue. While many Indonesians generally concede large-scale retrenchments, extensive retraining programmes, and massive increases in salary levels are essential prerequisites for improving the efficiency and effectiveness of the administration, none of these measures appears likely in the immediate future. Suharto did play with the idea of government departments laying off excessive staff for up to two years while still keeping them on payrolls with full public service privileges. Regulations to this effect were introduced, and a few employees were told not to report to work, but as political reaction against the moves began to gain momentum, Suharto had to be content with a ban on new staff, and various incentive schemes for improving performance. Suharto has also tried to raise salaries to more realistic levels but this is still well beyond the current capacity of the Indonesian economy, especially in view of the excessive numbers of public servants. As a result, corruption and bribery are likely to remain among the disabling features of a cumbersome administration for many years to come.

The problem of the army involves inter-unit conflict and rivalries, and various vested financial interests. Among the most powerful élite pressure groups within the army are the accumulated interests of Java's three regional divisions: West Java's Siliwangi, Central Java's Diponegoro, and East Java's Brawidjaja. Of these, the most highly organized is probably the Siliwangi's BPC: a powerful network of regional political, economic and military interests controlled by present and past members of the division. Likewise, the 'Brawidjaja Family' – the 'old boy's' association of the Brawidjaja – is a highly influential regional body with economic interests extending even into the Sulawesi's lucrative copra trade. Apart from preserving and promoting their power within the regions, an important concern of these organizations – which have emerged in all regional military districts – focuses on lobbying for central army staff posts and other 'plum' military, political and economic appointments, since these positions are clearly important in maintaining and extending the power and influence of the 'old boy' networks that each organization fosters. And while during the post-*coup* period the interests of the Diponegoro 'family' have been well served through Suharto and his key personal aides, keen rivalry developed especially between the Brawidjaja and Siliwangi.

During 1967 and 1968, conflicting military interests became closely intertwined with the wide-ranging political activities of the Siliwangi-led army and civilian radicals. Spearheaded largely by the Siliwangi's hawkish commander, Major General H. Dharsono, and the commander of the Army's Strategic Reserve (KOSTRAD), Major General (later Lieutenant General) Kemal Idris, these activities exacerbated traditional ethnic, social, cultural and religious hostilities, and by the eve of the 1968 con-

145

gress had earned the enmity of most of the main political, economic and military power groups within ruling circles. They had quite early made enemies of elements of the Nationalist Party by cracking down on the party in parts of Java and Sumatra. They had forced most other established party leaders into opposition by pressing for a 'two-party' system of government which transparently aimed at gradually undermining the remaining powers of the old political figures. They had aligned most of the army's vested economic interests against them by circulating a 'black list' of 'corrupt generals', and especially earned the ire of two financially powerful figures, Major General (later Lieutenant General) Ibnu Sutowo, and Major General Alamsjah. And they had assured themselves of the hostility of most traditional Javanese military and civilian leaders not only by the vigorous, strident (and therefore 'non-Oriental') style of their campaign, but also by their close connections with elements of the 'dissolved' Socialist Party (PSI), and pro-Western, 'progressive' outlook.

For Suharto, who needed the support of all these groups to reconfirm the legitimacy of his leadership, there was no alternative but to resist the demands of the Siliwangi-led 'hawks' (who, among other things, wanted Sukarno brought to trial and a sharp line drawn between the 'old' and 'new order' forces). This provoked bitter clashes during closed-door congressional discussions between previously staunch supporters of Suharto and his aides, and left Dharsono and Kemal Idris living on borrowed time in their commands. Further, the support these two leaders had previously enjoyed among similarly minded army generals, including Ishak Djuarsa, Witono, Solichin and Sarwo Edhie, faded discreetly into the background.

But Suharto's control over the army is not such that he can easily discipline influential generals who have incurred his displeasure. He has to seek agreement within the army leadership, much as elsewhere. In private, he often tacitly recognizes this problem by referring to 'my generals' rather than to 'the army'. He confronts the same problem when attempting to curb corruption within the officer corps. Whatever his personal attitude, he may often be forced to view excesses and abuses of power with a 'blind eye', or, at least, move with the utmost caution. This is especially true where financial interests are concerned since Suharto often needs the support of 'financial generals' (even more than the agreement of political leaders) to cut across the bottle-necks and 'red tape' of moribund, faction-ridden bureaucratic machinery. He must have funds to bridge the huge gap between army budgetary needs and the official government allocation, as well as for emergency funds to help quell unexpected political crises. He also knows that he cannot remove certain powerful generals from their posts without impairing his control over the military machine. And he has no guarantee that others who might take their place will be any less corrupt, more able, or as loyal to his leadership. If he is to make changes, he must normally move slowly, carefully choosing the time to strike.

Rule by 'consensus' in Indonesia's highly complex political environment not only involves knowing how the 'game' is played, but also who holds the trump cards. Rarely do political events flow from bold, clear-cut action, but rather are the outcome of a protracted cat-and-mouse game between contesting forces. The fact that the 'new order' hawks, Dharsono and Kemal Idris, held their commands for another twelve months following the stormy 1968 session of congress partly illustrates this point. And such was the trail of confusion surrounding their transfer to other posts that any of a number of reasons could have been responsible, including the official claim that they were merely moved in a 'routine tour of duty'. In this way, no one loses too much 'public face', and most of the defeated live to fight another day.

Several factors encourage this kind of manipulative politics. Among these are a rumour-prone public, a 'hungry' partisan press of varying quality, and the proliferation of intelligence 'operatives' and purveyors of *info* (as the Indonesians sometimes call the mixture of fact and fiction that is often circulated deliberately to confuse and bamboozle political opponents and the general public). Neither the public, press, nor the government can escape a share of the blame. Often, it seems, the wilder and more outrageous an accusation or story, the more chance it has of being believed. Only a handful of about thirty different papers published in Jakarta appear to check their information, and some will publish the most libellous material with a metaphorical 'believe-it-or-not' shrug of the shoulders. And government officials and military spokesmen sometimes seem to lack any real concern for accuracy or truth when making statements. As rumours run wild, they may even help fan them by providing cryptic comments full of misleading innuendoes.

Often, too, the twists and turns within the corridors of power stem from the constantly shifting patterns of alliances that form and reform. All the major political forces are thoroughly faction-ridden, and internal disputes – for example, the power struggles within political parties and other bodies – frequently become closely intertwined with broader political struggles between the major groups. Generally also, the various centres of power – economic, military and political – align and realign in such a way that no single interest can gain sufficient dominance to threaten the continued existence of the others.

Each vested interest also jealously guards – and attempts to preserve and expand – its own little empire so that efforts to institutionalize power invariably fail. This was among the reasons for the failure of parliamentary government in the fifties, and it continues to be an obstacle to establishing effective institutional government. Most likely this is because the institutionalization of power involves partly spelling out, in effect, who has lost and won in the 'power game' (through the specific rules and regulations governing the workings of the institutions), and this, the would-be losers will not allow. As a result, institutions such as parliament and congress fail as effective repositories of real power, becoming instead largely facades, or stages, for giant 'shadow plays' between contending forces. And the most important political action still proceeds beyond the reach of public scrutiny – often precipitated by men like the 'man from Raden Saleh street' – as the major decisions are made behind the scenes by the 'king makers' among the élite forces. This partly accounts for the apparent capriciousness and unpredictability of Indonesian politics. It also contributes towards one of the major obstacles to an understanding of political developments – simply determining 'where the action is'.

*

Is then Indonesia currently ungovernable by conventional means? Under Guided Democracy, congress, parliament, cabinet and other impressive institutions had little power. Most of the important decisions were made by small élite committees, such as KOTI (Supreme Operational Command), which was first formed early in 1962, ostensibly to meet the crisis situation brought about by the campaign to recover West Irian. After the successful conclusion of the campaign, KOTI was retained, and its activities expanded. During 1963 and 1964, KOTI came to play a major part in Sukarno's efforts to disperse military power, shifting it often into younger, more ambitious hands which could be more easily persuaded to accept his leadership without question or hesitation. During Malaysian confrontation, the body was renamed KOGAM (The Command for Crushing Malaysia), and after the *coup* was eventually disbanded with a pledge from Suharto to restore power to the appropriate institutions. Under Sukarno the implementation of policy, and the generation of public 'support', was also often in the hands of intelligence bodies like Subandrio's BPI, and the professional agitators and manipulators of the various mass organizations. That similar trends and patterns should have been continued into the post-*coup* period,

149

despite efforts to restore the effectiveness of institutional procedures, is primarily a consequence of the problems outlined above.

Even so, two distinguished Indonesian leaders who remain optimistic about the possibility of developing better government are Sudjatmoko, and the Minister of Trade, Sumitro Djojohadikusumo. Sudjatmoko, who was appointed Indonesian Ambassador to the United States in 1968, favours a 'strong executive' and a 'freely organized body politic, as well as a strongly development orientated leadership for both'. So far, however, the Indonesian political community has tended to remain mainly concerned about its sectional interests. Sumitro believes the success of the Suharto administration will depend on four 'indispensable ingredients': a 'framework of effective power, political perception, technical competence, and a deep sense of responsibility for the public interest'. He finds these ingredients present with the army providing the framework of effective power for better or for worse with all its deficiencies', and a 'relatively high degree of (political) perception prevalent among students' action groups, intellectuals, and political parties, as well as military leaders'. But he believes that success will depend on whether or not 'patriotic factions who are deeply concerned with the future of the country' are able to assert and maintain roles of dominance, and whether the 'appropriate balance' will be found and kept between the 'four ingredients'. If not, Sumitro asserts, any success and stability the Suharto administration achieves will be both 'temporary and precarious'.

As far as a framework of effective power is concerned, possibly two of the most important instruments at Suharto's disposal are the KOPKAMTIB and KORAMIL. The KORAMIL is part of the army's territorial management, and has already been discussed (p. 97). It has led to army involvement in all aspects of public life at village level, and, according to some officers, is potentially an instrument for tight army political control, making its leadership less dependent on the 'consensus' of the political parties. The KOPKAMTIB (The Operational Command for the Restoration of Security and Order) was formed under Suharto's emergency powers following the attempted *coup*, and has probably become the country's most powerful inquisitorial agency. It apparently has almost unlimited powers to investigate, apprehend, interrogate and 'screen' both military and civilian personnel suspected of pro-communist or anti-government activities.

KOPKAMTIB's continuing purge of *coup* and pro-*coup* suspects often accounts for the recurring uneasy climate that prevails within ruling circles. Few prominent officials apparently are beyond suspicion. Early in 1969, for instance, more than three years after the *coup*, the long arm of KOPKAMTIB reached in to the very summit of BAKIN and placed its head, Brigadier General Sudirgo, under detention. Informers like 'Jimmy' often lead to these arrests. Jimmy proved so successful as an informant for KOPKAMTIB – helping in the arrests of the communist leader Sudisman, Supardjo and Sjam (p. 75) and others – that he himself became a prime suspect, and eventually was arrested for having a long history of active involvement in the Communist Party. Meanwhile, according to press reports, Jimmy had gained promotion from lieutenant to captain for diligently performing his army tasks, and won a post-graduate university degree for a thesis entitled 'The Methods of Overcoming and of Eliminating the Communist Party in Indonesia'!

Together KOPKAMTIB and KORAMIL could prove formidable instruments in a 'big brother' type of political control but for the way inefficiency and intrigue tend to blunt the effectiveness of all the arms of authority in Indonesia – formal and informal. But they cannot be expected to promote a favourable climate for better government, and their activities and powers are already causing widespread concern among civilians. Likewise military control within the conventional administrative apparatus often is far more substantial than the six military ministers (as against seventeen civilians) might suggest. A breakdown of senior positions within the eighteen government departments gave the following picture at the end of 1970: – Inspector-Generals (an army innovation to improve efficiency), eight military and four civilian; Secretary-Generals, seven military and ten civilian; and Director-Generals, twenty-five military and thirty-seven civilian.

*

Between pre- and post-*coup* Indonesia, however, there are some striking differences in the style of presidential leadership. Like Sukarno, Suharto has a great desire to be well thought of among his people, but in markedly different ways. In contrast to the exuberant Sukarno, Suharto – or 'Pak Harto' as he is commonly known among Indonesians – is a shy, friendly man whose mild manner often belies his inner toughness and resolution.

During 1969, Suharto kindly agreed to my request that he set down in writing an outline of his philosophy of life. His reply revealed the strong influence of his Javanese heritage and his deep spirituality and sincerity – characteristics commonly remarked upon by those who meet him. He wrote of the need of man to realize relationships with all mankind and with God as the great creator. He said the deeper a person's faith then the closer that person was to God, and the better able to retain a calm, composed spirit and a clear, cool head in confronting life's daily problems, whether big or small. Javanese parents, he noted, especially instruct their children never to be surprised, never to be disappointed, and never to wrongly use power. But whether or not one was capable of receiving God's guidance depended on one's disposition, and this involved purifying one's thoughts, feelings and desires. And in this way, one could carry out one's duties in life by truth, goodness, justice and well-being towards others.

As might be expected from a man holding these views, Suharto emerges as a restrained, cautious leader. He is often characterized in the Indonesian press as one who 'makes haste slowly' and avoids the 'spectacular'. He admits he prefers to remain silent until his efforts have produced results (often a necessary precaution if they are not to be dexterously negated), and that his opponents frequently take advantage of his silence. He also stresses his concern for 'harmony', which may partly account for his being regarded as a 'centrist', or a 'middle-of-the-roader'. 'In our culture,' Suharto asserts, 'harmony is regarded as the most essential value; harmony between man and society, between man and God.' He also does not agree that traditional values must be destroyed before modernization can begin. 'The problem is not to destroy traditional values but to adjust them to the demands of development.' And this, he adds, 'is not purely an economic affair. The economy is but an aspect, although a fundamental aspect, in the process of nation building. The important things are not just economic ends, but the release of the creative energies of a nation, and the mobilization of the will and determination of that nation in the pursuit of new goals.'

In this light, Suharto has firm views on the kind of leadership Indonesia needs. 'The essence of leadership,' he told me, 'is really the ability to solve problems which the community confronts, to point out ways of overcoming them, and to point out the way to a future together, and to get the community moving to carry things out. Because of this, a leader must foremost possess two qualities: firstly, an understanding of the outlook or view of life of the community itself; and secondly, an understanding of conditions within the community.'

To awaken the people's spirit and stimulate the community to action, Suharto continued, a leader must set a good example. He must be cautious and wise, and have the courage both to supervise and give correction, as well as the ability to direct things along the right path when the community is inclined to deviate from the joint programme and national aims. 'For our nation, which is still developing, which still suffers a lack of skills, a leader must also get the right priorities in national activities. And in his position as a leader, he especially must have an attitude of behaviour which is sincere and not excessive. Because what we carry out is the result of joint discussions, then to achieve this aim together, it is also necessary to have honesty and loyalty – whether from the leader to the community, or from the community to the leader, or among the community. Finally, because our development must be progressive, every leader – at all levels – must possess the benevolence to surrender his leadership eventually and give experience to the oncoming generation.'

Many people will argue over the extent Suharto may have succeeded in achieving ideals such as these during the early years of his stewardship. His supporters may point to aspects of his leadership, such as the improved functioning of cabinet, and contrast this with the era of Sukarno rule. Under Guided Democracy, the cabinet not only eventually reached the ludicrous total of 100 ministers, but also served as little more than a forum for the political speeches of Sukarno and Subandrio.

Under Suharto, cabinet has regained much of its intended function. It meets monthly to hear the reports of ministers heading departments and to discuss general national problems and policy. An inner cabinet meets twice monthly to deal with more concrete problems. Its membership will vary, depending on the matters under discussion. Non-cabinet members will be included as the circumstances require. For example, if security questions are involved, the deputy commander of KOPKAMTIB, Lieutenant General Sumitro, and the head of BAKIN, Major General Sutopo Juwono, will be among those present. Weekly meetings are also held by a tightly knit economic stabilization committee, and less commonly, a similar committee dealing with political stability may also convene. At all meetings, Suharto encourages short, pointed reports, and insists that firm decisions are reached. His grasp of detail generally keeps ministers and assistants on their toes, and he has won respect for his ability to hear out various points of view, sum up concisely, and quickly reach a decision. His energetic, youthful-looking, secretary of cabinet, Brigadier General Sudharmono, has also brought to this office a degree of efficiency and order that was hitherto absent.

Suharto has also shown a capacity for doing his 'home-work' that Sukarno never quite attained. Pre-occupied with politics, Sukarno gave little attention to administrative procedures, and a hopelessly chaotic administrative situation developed, especially in the office of the presidency. Suharto has made efforts to rectify this, and has also introduced procedures for administrative control in all government departments. But the plight of the bureaucracy is such that these measures will probably take a long time to establish effectively.

Even so, Suharto's critics wonder whether the commendable aspects of his leadership – and especially his concern for economic reform and development – will not ultimately be overshadowed by what they view as his shortcomings. Among other things, they point to his apparent inability to curb the greed of some of his close aides, as well as to an alleged 'timidity' in effecting necessary reforms. He is also frequently accused of being a man of 'reaction' rather than 'action' – a criticism he finds especially irksome. He argues he acts according to carefully conceived strategies which he cannot disclose. Periodically, too, he comes under attack for inept handling of the communications media, and sometimes for a consequent 'credibility' gap. A dull, dreary speaker, he also suffers badly in comparison with Sukarno's dynamic oratorical skills.

Prominent Indonesians have also become concerned by what they regard as a lack of 'national purpose' in his leadership. 'Suharto has no dream to lead the country,' one eminent civilian told me in confidence in 1969. 'This is his proud boast. It's meant to reflect upon all that was wrong with Sukarno and his vainglory and ambition. But is it an advantage or a disadvantage? Indonesian people still need spiritual leadership. They still need charisma.' The chairman of Congress, General Nasution, also told me in mid-1969: 'Indonesian government today is too pragmatic – too much concerned with bread and butter issues ... this is a reaction against the Sukarno period, but it has swung too far. There is an imbalance again, and sometime in the future, this imbalance will have to be corrected. We can't go on ignoring ideological issues.'

Other criticisms against Suharto involving the 'rationality' of his leadership especially arouse his anger. He is accused by some of an undue reliance on 'spiritual advisers'. One of his ASPRI is even called the 'minister for mystical affairs'. His close friends, however, vigorously deny these allegations. Usually, also, the stories involving such charges are vague, and open to differing interpretations. For example, Suharto is supposed to have settled on a figure of twenty-four cabinet ministers after a *guru* (spiritual adviser) recommended this as an 'auspicious number'. (Cabinet was later reduced to twenty-three, although the deputy commander of the armed forces also had a quasi-cabinet status as a Minister of State). Another story insists Suharto expended some considerable effort gaining custody of a sacred drum which was supposed to provide a 'magical 1,000 days of special grace'. Most Indonesians have a mystical bent, and undoubtedly these beliefs have an important influence on their everyday lives. But there is a lack of convincing evidence that Suharto's mystical leanings carry an inordinate weight in his decision-making.

Perhaps the most telling comment on Suharto's leadership is the lack of serious alternative possible candidates for the presidency. It is not a job that anyone could lightly undertake, and certainly not without the support of the military establishment. And while there are highly ambitious men within the army who might entertain the possibility of one day making a bid for power, it is unlikely that any could become a serious contender for the throne in the more immediate future. The American commentator, Willard Hanna, may well be right in asserting: 'Pak Harto, it seems, not only almost inadvertently fell into the job; he is also stuck with it.'

Chapter 8

Communism Since the *Coup*

At the risk of over-simplification, three further issues, perhaps, especially threaten Indonesian stability during the coming years, and the prospects of its people being able to dispel the spectre of a dark and gloomy future. Of these, the 'communist issue' is discussed below. The 'religious issue' is dealt with in Chapter 9. And, finally, Chapter 10 examines the complex conflict between the forces of tradition and those representing change.

*

'If I die,' declared the Indonesian Communist Party (PKI) leader, Sudisman, during his trial before a military court in Jakarta in July 1967, 'this will not mean the death of the Communist Party. Although the Communist Party has been smashed to pieces ... this is only a temporary defeat. The Communist Party will rise again.' Sudisman – who was executed in October 1968 – was one of five key leaders responsible for building the Communist Party into the most formidable political organization in Indonesia by the eve of the 1965 attempted *coup*. The other four, chairman D. N. Aidit, Lukman, Njoto and Sakirman, had earlier shared the fate of countless thousands of party members and supporters who were among those massacred in the brutal blood-letting that swept parts of the archipelago following the *coup*. Scores of thousands more were also thrown into prisons throughout the country. But even greater numbers avoided either capture or death, and survived to inherit a legacy of blood and hate.

Today, the very reasons for the Party's earlier rise to prominence, the circumstances of its defeat, and the seemingly insoluble nature of so many of Indonesia's social and economic problems together lend credibility to Sudisman's assertions that the Communist Party will rise again. However, the more immediate concern is with the political and economic turbulence the remnants of the Party can possibly create.

The Party Aidit led during the fifties and early sixties was itself reborn from a bloodbath and purge following the 1948 uprising in Madiun, East Java. Only sketchy information is available about that event, but it would seem to bear a striking parallel with the aftermath of the 1965 attempted *coup*. The communist and left-wing elements who made a bid for power during the Madiun affair especially singled out the most dedicated, orthodox Muslims as their targets among the communities over which they briefly gained control. Their brutality as they shot, burned, or hacked these people to death, destroying their houses, mosques and religious schools, was matched only by the viciousness of the reprisals launched by Islamic elements when government forces regained control of the region. An American scholar, Robert Jay, who conducted field research in the area five years after the event, found the local people were still overwhelmed by recollections of the ferocity and extent of the killings. In one city of 50,000 alone, to the south of Madiun, government officials estimated that half of the male population caught in the city had been killed.

The growth of the Communist Party following independence far outstripped that of other political parties. From less than 8,000 members early in 1952, the Party emerged as the fourth largest in the 1955 elections (trailing only the Nationalist Party (PNI), the Masjumi and the Religious Scholars League (NU)) with more than six million votes, and over sixteen per cent of the total cast. In local elections held throughout Java two years later, the Party increased its share of the vote by more than one-third, making heavy inroads into the following of the Nationalist Party. But its most spectacular growth came during the early sixties under Guided Democracy, when most of its strongest civilian opposition was either outlawed or severely curtailed. The strongly anti-communist Masjumi, which had polled nearly eight million votes during the 1955 elections, and the small, but influential Indonesian Socialist Party (PSI) were both 'dissolved' by Sukarno in 1960 for their involvement in the 1958 rebellion. Given protection from army repression also by Sukarno, and aided by his 'revolutionary' stress, the Party grew to claim a membership of about three million by mid-1964, and another fifteen million among its affiliated mass organizations of youth, labour, women, farmers, and so forth. Efforts among anti-communist elements of Indonesian society to block its continuing growth (such as the Body for the Promotion of Sukarnoism (BPS) formed late in 1964) invariably ended in failure. Even its diminutive rival, the Murba party, was declared inactive early in 1965, and the leadership of other parties such as the Nationalist Party assumed an increasingly pro-communist outlook. Increasingly also, the Communist Party acquired, for some observers, the image of 'heir-apparent' to Sukarno, and the only force capable of coping with the country's political and economic problems.

The Communist Party's power in the pre-*coup* period flowed from several sources. Among other things, its organization and militancy were unmatched among the other major political groupings. Whatever its internal dissensions, the leadership maintained an outward appearance of cohesion and purpose. And whereas the leadership of most major political parties had increasingly become divorced from the masses they claimed to represent, the Communist Party retained and extended its close contact among the people. Not having shared the 'fruits of independence' to the extent of other parties – at least at national level through lucrative ministerial and commercial appointments – its leaders also retained a reputation for honesty and dedication that contrasted with the general corruption and hypocrisy of post-independence politics in Indonesia. But more especially, the Party's platform and ability to focus attention on the needs of the underprivileged – the landless peasants, the urban poor, the underpaid civil servants – encouraged a growing conviction among many Indonesians that it alone could provide the leadership and dynamism needed to bring about the 'just and prosperous' society for which millions yearned.

The Communist Party's pre-*coup* success also helped pave the way for its post-*coup* annihilation. Through threatening the established domestic power structure, the Party polarized powerful opposition within both military and civilian circles. The more covert moves of the army leadership to meet the rising power of the Party were briefly outlined in Chapter 3 (pp. 69-71). But what especially helped prime the fuse for the wave of post-*coup* killings were the deep hostilities Communist Party agitation had provoked in overcrowded rural regions, especially through inciting violent conflict between the landless and Muslim and Nationalist Party landowners. Even before the *coup*, armed bands of Muslims were striking back at communists. And in the wake of the *coup*, with army support, killings began almost immediately in the most strongly Muslim province of Atjeh, and quickly spread in East Java and parts of Central Java. Frequently, the killings acquired religious sanction as a 'Holy War', with the communists regarded as the 'infidels', and their death a means by which a Muslim ensured his salvation. But anti-communist nationalist elements and Christians also joined in the atrocities. And while much of the responsibility for the slaughter must rest with the army, there is little doubt that the Communist Party caught the backlash of the profound economic, social, spiritual and psychological tensions it had helped crystallize within Indonesian society in its efforts to rise to power.

Just how many people died – or how many of these were communists – can never really be known with any accuracy. The official figure of 78,000 can almost certainly be discounted as too low. Likewise, estimates of about one million are probably inflated. According to these figures, in certain parts of Central and East Java almost one-third of the population was killed, but there is no evidence of killings having occurred on that scale. Probably estimates ranging from between 150,000 and 300,000 are closer the truth, but this cannot alter the fact that both the nature and scope of the killings were such that they could only have left a long-lasting, traumatic legacy among hundreds of thousands of people.

Just how many hard core party members survived the purge also cannot be known with any certainty. As became apparent following the *coup*, army intelligence on the activities of the Communist Party was extremely poor and unco-ordinated. Even the backgrounds of quite prominent figures remain unknown to KOPKAMTIB (The Command for the Restoration of Security and Order) – the responsible authority for ensuring that communist power does not rise again. But according to KOPKAMTIB sources, about ten per cent (300,000) of the Party's total membership of three million could be classed as cadres. Of this number, probably more than 200,000 survived both the killings and the mass arrests. Among about 120,000 suspects held in prisons at one stage following the *coup*, only about 20,000 were found to be cadres and key leaders. And of party members that received quite extensive training, although not to cadre level, KOPKAMTIB estimates that perhaps 1,400,000 remain at large throughout the archipelago.

The covert efforts of Communist Party remnants to regroup following the purge and the ban imposed on the Party in March 1966 are even more difficult to unravel. Sudisman led one attempt before his capture in December 1966. What headway he made is far from clear, but the direction towards which he had hoped to lead a revitalized party was evident from a 'self-criticism' of the party found among documents in his possession at the time of his arrest.[1]

1. 'Set up a Marxist-Leninist PKI to lead the Democratic Revolutionary People of Indonesia', (Self-Criticism of the PKI Central Committee Politbureau), dated Central Java, September 1966.

In this analysis of where the party had gone wrong (Sudisman acknowledged its authenticity during his trial), surviving leaders conceded that they had erred in failing to fully evaluate their own weaknesses, as well as the strength of their opponents. The 'self-criticism' argued that the Party had grown too fast, its organization had become too loose, discipline too lax, and links with the masses too tenuous. It had also become too closely linked with Sukarno, and too preoccupied with the struggle against 'imperialism' at the expense of promoting the class struggle within Indonesia.

According to the document, the remedy lay in forsaking the 'peaceful' road to power that the Party had pursued under Aidit, and adopting a three-pronged strategy involving the rebuilding of a 'purified' Marx-Leninist party, the promotion of an armed 'people's struggle' (peasants led by workers) in an anti-feudal agrarian revolution, and the development of a revolutionary united front between workers and peasants under working class leadership. The 'self-criticism' commented:

The Party's past experiences show the importance of staunch Marx-Leninists defending Marx-Leninism and opposing modern revisionism, studying the teachings of Marx, Engels, Lenin and Stalin, and making a special study of the thoughts of MAO TSE TUNG which have had glorious results in defending and developing Marx-Leninism and bringing it to its peak in the present era . . .

And lest there still be doubts that the new Communist Party would look to Peking rather than Moscow, the analysis declared that the core of 'modern revisionism' was found in the Soviet Communist Party, and could not be fought while maintaining friendships with 'modern revisionists'.

During 1968, military authorities smashed what they claimed was an attempt to organize a Maoist-style armed uprising among the people of Central and East Java. Throughout the two provinces, communists had formed what they called 'project committees'. These were established in mountainous regions as bases from which to organize and co-ordinate a 'people's liberation army'. Basic military training allegedly was being provided by a number of special schools modelled on North Vietnamese military methods. According to the army, a team of Communist Party cadres had gone to Hanoi in 1964 to study guerrilla tactics, and some of these had returned to organize similar training schools in Central and East Java. The aim was eventually to have trained men in every village. Some of these would be part of mobile guerrilla detachments, while others would belong to village units. The provinces had also been zoned according to the degree of influence the Party exerted into 'red' (under party control), 'white' (disputed) and 'green' (army control) areas. Communist Party tactics were to work out from the 'red' areas, changing 'white' to 'red' and 'green' to 'white' through propaganda, agitation and exploiting tensions and grievances within the communities. To win the confidence of the village, communist cadres practiced the 'three togethers' – working with the villagers, eating with them, and sleeping in the villages.

According to the army, the Party had established its headquarters in a bleak, isolated wasteland south of the East Java town of Blitar. An army sweep through the area in mid-1968 uncovered scores of Viet Cong-style underground hide-outs, smashed organized detachments of the 'people's liberation army', and led to the seizure of a motley collection of small arms and a few hand-grenades. Among some 850 communists either captured or killed during the military operation were more than twenty prominent figures who had successfully eluded the army dragnet since the attempted *coup*. Three of these, Olean Hutapea, a former central committee member and editor of the Party's main theoretical journal 'Red Star', Rewang (alias Karto), the former Central Java district committee chairman, and Ruslan Widjajasastra, the former East Java district committee chairman, were believed by the army to have assumed main responsibility for the Party's leadership following Sudisman's capture in December 1966.

The real threat the Communist Party posed during 1968 is difficult to assess. The months leading up to the South Blitar military operation had been marked by rising terrorism in parts of Central and East Java. Muslim religious leaders and village officials had especially become the target of kidnappings and killings. A number of soldiers had also been assassinated. Other causes of serious concern were the defections of military personnel and terrorist attacks on civil defence outposts and arms' depots. Reports concerning the extent of military defections invariably were contradictory, and the army vigorously denied one story claiming a mass walk-out of 300 troops from an East Java unit.

But government concern over the general security situation was clear from the continuing arrests and purges of communist and pro-communist suspects among the ranks of the military and civil bureaucracy in Central and East Java. Both bodies were known to be heavily infiltrated by the Communist Party and pro-communist Nationalist Party elements, and, as a result, their loyalty to the Suharto administration was open to question. Nor could there be any doubt that general dissatisfaction and unrest were widespread among many communities in these overcrowded, increasingly impoverished provinces. But the likelihood of a 'people's liberation army' operating successfully in Central and East Java seems rather remote. Most of the region is easily accessible and provides no real refuge for secure guerrilla bases. And the ease with which the army overcame party resistance in South Blitar, and the meagre arms' finds during the operation, suggests that the Party had made little headway in its preparations for a 'comeback' and had certainly not solved the crucial problem of getting adequate supplies of arms, ammunition and funds.

A more substantial military problem posed by communist insurgency in the post-*coup* period emerged not from Communist Party remnants but from Sarawakian Chinese along the border region of West Kalimantan (Borneo). During 1963, about 1000 young Chinese crossed into Indonesian territory from Sarawak (of whom Lai Pa Ka was one, see pp. 43-7) and offered themselves as 'volunteers' in the Indonesian campaign to 'crush' Malaysia. Most were members of the Chinese-dominated Sarawak United People's Party (SUPP) which also opposed the formation of Malaysia. However, the SUPP was then heavily infiltrated by the underground Sarawak Communist Organization (SCO) – known among members simply as the 'Organization' or 'O' – and many of the young 'volunteers' were also members of the 'Organization's' illegal Sarawak Advanced Youth Association (SAYA). The youths were given military training by the Indonesian armed forces and regrouped into several units with colourful names like the 'black panthers', 'white panthers', and so on. But by the time of the attempted *coup* in 1965, following further reorganizations, most were found among one of two units – the Sarawak People's Guerrilla Movement (PGRS) and the North Kalimantan People's Army (PARAKU). Led by Wong Kie Hsui, Lai Pa Ka and others, the PGRS operated in the western sector of the border region with a strength of about 500. The PARAKU, with a strength variously estimated from 150 to 250 and led by Wong Kie Tjek (who had been deported from Kuching in 1961 for alleged communist activities, and had then gone to Peking) occupied the remote eastern sector of the border. About October 1966, following the reversal of the Indonesian government's policy of confrontation against Malaysia, at least two other leading Sarawakian communist figures – Yap Chung Hoo and Lai Choon – joined the PGRS and began developing the border region as a guerrilla base for terrorist activities against Sarawak.

The first clash between the guerrillas and Indonesian forces came during July 1967 when PGRS units attacked an air force depot at Sanggau Ledo, inland from the West Kalimantan coastal town of Singkawang. Killing four Indonesians during the raid, the guerrillas seized nearly 200 weapons and 20,000 rounds of ammunition which they used to establish new armed units formed from among about 2,000 locally recruited Chinese.

Moving in more than 6,000 troops from other parts of the archipelago to supplement the province's regular territorial forces, the Indonesian army began disrupting the guerrilla's sources of food, and isolating them in remote, mountainous terrain. By mid-1969, army authorities claimed they had successfully broken the strength of the PGRS and began patrols against the PARAKU in the remote inland border area.

However, the Indonesian army – which now co-operates closely with Malaysian security forces – is unlikely to be able to completely eliminate guerrilla forces along the border. Much of the region is sparsely populated, communications are poor, and the guerrillas have little difficulty getting new recruits and supplies, including food, medical needs, and money, from the extensive and highly organized communist underground network of the 'Organization' in Sarawak across the border.

Communist insurgency in West Kalimantan also had wider repercussions. In October 1967, a bitter clash erupted between inland Dyaks and Chinese. Several hundred Chinese were slaughtered and about 50,000 were forced to flee their hinterland farms, shops and businesses for the security of coastal towns. Military authorities claim PGRS guerrillas triggered the clash by killing Dyaks who refused to co-operate with them and by looting Dyak villages. But some Chinese allege that Dyak political interests with army backing provoked the fighting in a deliberate effort to drive the Chinese from the hinterland. Whatever the truth, the outcome suited the army's short-term aims of limiting the support the guerrillas could hope to receive from both Dyaks and local Chinese in inland areas. It also played into the hands of Dyaks who viewed the prosperity of the hard-working Chinese with covetous eyes. But the episode paralyzed the region's economy, and embittered thousands of Chinese who lost everything they owned and found themselves herded into camps near the coastal towns of Pontianak, Singkawang and Mempawah.

It is difficult to assess the consequences of these events. Chinese migration to the region dates back several centuries. Before the arrival of Dutch military power during the early nineteenth century, Chinese virtually ruled large enclaves through the organization of close-knit communal bodies called *kongsis*. Although the Dutch smashed these, the Chinese continued to dominate the economy. They worked as miners, farmers, traders, builders, shopkeepers and so on. They provided the know-how that developed the region. They also intermarried with the indigenous people, and especially with the Dyaks.

Today, Chinese account for an estimated twenty-five per cent of West Kalimantan's population of about two million, and their birth rate is among the highest. In some major towns, such as Singkawang, more than two-thirds of the population is Chinese. And their ties with the indigenous people are often closer than many Indonesian military and civilian administrators from Jakarta can hope to achieve. Thus by failing to maintain law and order in the province, military authorities have most probably aided communist insurgency in the long-term through alienating a significant sector of the population and seriously impairing economic development in the region.

While the Communist Party was not notably strong in West Kalimantan before the *coup*, Sarawakian security officials believe that the 'Organization' is now well established in the province, and is working with remnants of the Communist Party. A senior Chinese security official I interviewed in Kuching in 1969 told me that possibly two-thirds of the 'Organization's' leadership probably remained more or less permanently in West Kalimantan.

With long experience working underground, these key men kept in the shadows, using figures like Wong Kie Tjek, who leads the PARAKU, as 'front men'. The same official told me that he did not believe that the defector Lai Pa Ka had 'changed his colours' – only his tactics. And although Indonesian authorities have used Lai Pa Ka in their efforts to persuade other guerrillas to defect, the report of his interrogation, which I was allowed to read, tends to support this view. 'By surrendering,' said the report of the military police, 'we believe he hopes to be able to continue to help the PGRS struggle indirectly.' However, Indonesian authorities refused a Malaysian request for Lai Pa Ka's extradition to Sarawak for further interrogation.

It is this combination of Communist Party and Chinese influences that many Indonesians apparently fear most. Especially within army circles, the country's Chinese population, totalling about three million, the Communist Party and China's potential influence in the region, are seen as essentially interdependent parts of the same communist problem. And because West Kalimantan has a high proportion of Chinese, is close to other Chinese strongholds in Southeast Asia, and has easier access to Peking, it is viewed with special concern. Some army officers even claim the strategy of the post-*coup* communist insurgency in the province aimed at involving large numbers of Indonesian armed forces in guerrilla warfare so that the communist underground could operate under less pressure in Java. According to this view, the communist movement was pursuing a 'two front' strategy. The outer 'front' linking Singapore with Pontianak in West Kalimantan, and with Medan in North Sumatra, operated under direct control from Peking through Singapore. The inner 'front', centred in Java and led by former Communist Party leaders, had more difficult communication and logistic problems to contend with, but still received funds and other supplies from Peking through Indonesian Chinese.

*

The history of Sino-Indonesian relations reflects the fluctuating political fortunes of anti-Chinese elements within Indonesian society. Despite early recognition of the Mao Tse Tung government in Peking in April 1950, no Indonesian ambassador was appointed to China until late in 1953 when the domestic power balance tipped away from the early pro-Western, Islam-oriented and anti-communist administrations in favour of the radical nationalists under Prime Minister Ali Sastroamidjojo. Eighteen months later, relations took a further significant step forward during the 1955 Afro-Asian conference in Bandung with agreement on the thorny question of the dual nationality of Chinese in Indonesia. However, ratification of the treaty was delayed until early in 1960 by the turbulent political conditions within the country in the late fifties. During this period, Peking actively courted Sukarno, quickly offering him an $11 million credit and strong political support against rebel movements in the Outer Islands, which included the anti-communist, Islamic elements. But by late in 1959, a tough anti-Chinese campaign to dislodge Chinese traders from rural regions had brought ties between Peking and Jakarta close to breaking point.

While the primary instigators of anti-Chinese activities in Indonesia have consistently been found among the strongly Islamic entrepreneurial groups and their right-wing military supporters, campaigns have always capitalized on widespread anti-Chinese sentiment. Underlying this feeling is a complex set of historical, political, economic and socio-cultural factors. Chinese are variously accused of having been 'colonial lackeys' and of siding with the Dutch during the independence struggle, of monopolizing key sectors of the economy and consequently exploiting Indonesians, of lacking patriotism and owing allegiance either to Peking or Taipei, of 'cultural arrogance' and general 'attitudes of superiority', and of numerous other unlikeable traits. On the other hand, many Indonesians find much to admire about China, including its ancient culture, its size and importance in world affairs (especially since it is an Asian nation in a Western dominated world) and the industriousness of its people. But these same admirable features also help reinforce their fears.

Under Guided Democracy, Sukarno successfully curtailed anti-Chinese activity. He deftly brought the turbulent 1959/1960 campaign under control, and acted most forthrightly when further trouble erupted in May 1963 following a state visit by former Chinese President Liu Shao-ch'i. Bluntly accusing 'counter-revolutionary' domestic elements (including the outlawed Masjumi and Socialist Party) and 'foreign subversives' (meaning the US or CIA) of master-minding the events, he demonstrated the importance he attached to growing ties with China. By 1964, he not only had come to rely increasingly on Peking's support for his aggressive foreign policy, but some observers believed the two countries had reached an 'understanding' whereby they would co-operate to exclude Western influence from Asia, giving Indonesia hegemony in the 'Maphilindo' (Malaysia-Philippines-Indonesia) region. Whether or not this was so, Peking's hand in Indonesia was greatly strengthened by the preference the Communist Party began showing towards its claims to leadership of the international communist movement, and by the widening breach between Moscow and Jakarta. Moreover, by joining the élite 'nuclear club' in October 1964, Peking gained a major psychological advantage among Afro-Asian nations which, in the case of Indonesia, it quickly exploited by offering a $50 million credit late in 1964 and underwriting Sukarno's ambitious plans for a 'conference of new emerging forces' (CONEFO) in the shape of a rival United Nations.

Following the 1965 attempted *coup,* Sino-Indonesian relations dramatically sank to a new low. The Chinese embassy in Jakarta earned its first stiff rebuke from the Indonesian government by ignoring the period of national mourning declared for the murdered army generals. And as the anti-communist purge quickly gained momentum,

Peking's propaganda organs began churning out their choicest epithets to revile the 'Suharto-Nasution fascist militarist regime'. Within days of the *coup*, army backed newspapers were intimating that China and some Chinese living in Indonesia had provided both material and moral support for the *coup* leaders, and before long, both came under sharp attack from pro-army demonstrators, especially in Jakarta and Medan (North Sumatra).

Indonesian foreign office officials soon lost count of the number of protests Peking lodged during the next several months. Demands by demonstrators led to the closure of the well-staffed Jakarta bureau of the New China News Agency (NCNA) in March 1966. In April, military authorities began closing Chinese schools, and Chinese and their property continued to come under vigorous attack. In November 1967, with the Indonesian mission in Peking and the Chinese embassy in Jakarta reduced to embattled, tottering outposts, both countries withdrew the last of their diplomats and relations were formally 'suspended' or 'frozen' without a complete break being declared.

Pressure groups within Indonesia attempted to force a clean break in Sino-Indonesian relations, but neither the Indonesian nor the Chinese government wanted to go that far. Peking probably clung to the very slender hope that Sukarno might somehow still regain power. It also had to consider the interests of an estimated 250,000 Chinese citizens living in Indonesia, and a further four to five times that number holding neither Chinese nor Indonesian citizenship. Some of the so-called 'stateless' Chinese looked more to Taipei than Peking, however, and were among groups within Indonesia pressing for a complete break.

More than political considerations were at stake. Some pro-Taiwanese Chinese were also attempting to regain lucrative economic positions which they had lost progressively to pro-Peking Chinese since the late fifties. But while the new Indonesian administration was developing closer ties with Taiwan, it never seriously considered ex-

171

tending diplomatic recognition to Taipei rather than Peking. For both domestic and international reasons, the Suharto government did not want too violent a swing to the 'right' and the 'West'. It was also concerned that a complete break with Peking could lead to increased Chinese subversive activities in Indonesia.

*

Government policy towards China since the *coup* has generally aimed at keeping Peking from meddling in Indonesian domestic affairs. By and large, this policy appears to have been successful. Despite some public claims, there is a lack of tangible evidence that Peking has been able to give the shattered Indonesian Communist Party much more than moral support. During visits to both East Java and West Kalimantan in mid-1969, military authorities told me that while communications with Peking remained open – probably through Chinese businessmen – they did not have evidence that the Communist Party remnants had received significant material aid, especially when contrasted with the pre-*coup* period when funds (according to military sources) flowed through private Chinese banks into Communist Party coffers.

However, Peking has provided a sanctuary for a quasi-government in exile led by the surviving Communist Party politbureau member Jusuf Adjitorop, and including several Indonesian diplomats who refused to return to Jakarta following the *coup*. (Adjitorop, who has been in China since mid-1964, publicly foreshadowed the Indonesian Communist Party's Maoist strategy advocated by the 'self-criticism', discussed above, when he spoke at the fifth congress of the Albanian Workers' Party in November 1966). China has also continued its barrage of propaganda directed against the Suharto government through the powerful transmitters of Radio Peking, but by 1970, these broadcasts had adopted a somewhat softer line.

Since 1967, the Indonesian government has also made a concerted effort to contain anti-Chinese activity. Practical considerations alone dictate such a course. The government has pledged itself to improve economic conditions, and the Chinese still exert a crucial influence in the Indonesian economy. For instance, according to some sources, Chinese control from seventy to eighty per cent of money in circulation. They are also an important source of economic and technical skills. The country cannot afford the high cost of economic disruption already caused during the post-*coup* period by anti-Chinese measures in Atjeh, East Java, West Kalimantan, and other regions.

Even so, there are still a number of serious legacies to overcome. Among these is the treatment of the families of those who died in the post-*coup* killings. Apart from the economic hardships these families must suffer, their children are also often being denied schooling because of the involvement of one or more of the family in the Communist Party. 'Will they grow up an embittered, hate-filled generation sworn to avenge their fathers?' asked a Javanese in Jogjakarta, with whom I once discussed this problem. He thought it highly likely they would.

The plight of scores of thousands of political prisoners is another problem. Their fate has won wider attention than that of the hapless families, including the notice of the International Commission of Jurists. In September 1966, the Attorney-General Sugih Arto put the number of political prisoners at 120,000. They were being held in more than 350 detention camps and prisons throughout the country, and were classified into four groups. 'A' class prisoners were prominent Communist Party officials and *coup* leaders. Their total was generally given at between 4,500 to 5,000. 'B' class prisoners were allegedly known Communist Party cadres and activists, and these numbered about 15,000. 'C' and 'D' class prisoners were lesser party members and functionaries, or others suspected of limited involvement in subversive activities. Together they numbered about 100,000, of whom about half had been released by late in 1969 after lengthy periods of indoctrination.

Both the conditions under which political prisoners have been held and the injustice of detaining scores of thousands for long periods without trial have come under sharp attack. During February and March 1969, allegations of brutalities and killings among prisoners detained near the Central Javanese town of Purwodadi added a new and far graver dimension to these criticisms. While the army vigorously denied accusations that as many as 3,500 political prisoners had been massacred, it failed to allay suspicions by not forming an independent and impartial body to investigate the charges. The army has also been sharply criticized by the Indonesian press and elsewhere for its decision to establish isolated penal colonies for 'B' category prisoners. The first of these set up at Buru Island in the Moluccas for about 2,500 prisoners during 1969 quickly drew comparisons with the infamous Boven Digul – the West Irian exile to which the Dutch administration consigned political trouble-makers during the thirties.

These criticisms generally reflect a wider concern. For many civilians, in particular, the proper treatment of the Communist Party detainees has become one of several issues whereby the army's 'sense of justice' can itself be judged. If army authorities cannot persuade the general public that they are doing their utmost within the limits of a shortage of funds and inadequate judicial facilities to ensure that all political prisoners receive just and fair consideration, only the army's opponents and especially the remnants of the Communist Party will be the long-term beneficiaries. A great deal of uneasiness has already been caused by the tendency of some military authorities to exercise power in an arbitrary manner and to exploit the question of the Communist Party as a means of stifling criticism and diverting attention from their own short-comings.

Apart from the activities of the Communist Party remnants already outlined above, there have been endless rumours and reports of alleged Communist Party plots and communist subversion in the years since the *coup*. Some of these reports have been exposed as clearly false, while others must be treated with considerable scepticism. In mid-1968, for instance, the South Sulawesi military commander caused a stir with a claim that Peking-backed communist forces were operating in remote parts of the province. Subsequently, this alleged 'volunteer army' proved to be the bedraggled remnants of a fantastically anti-communist Islamic rebel movement. Similarly, on the eve of a presidential visit to Sumatra later the same year, the military commander in the central Sumatran region claimed to have smashed a 'communist' plot to establish a 'base area' in the Riau islands. When confronted by foreign journalists, including myself, the same military commander failed to substantiate his claims, yet early the following year was still telling the Indonesian press about 'communist activists' in the Riau who were trying to establish a 'people's army'.

Alleged Communist party 'plots' have also been a favourite pretext for justifying ongoing purges within military and civilian circles since the *coup*. Often those arrested have only remote or tenuous links with communism, and, in many instances, most probably have been 'Sukarnoists' or radical nationalists whose personal ambitions have caused uneasiness within the ranks of the present army and civilian leadership. Even business circles have resorted to similar tactics, as, for example, when the national airline, Garuda, linked the dismissal of about 1,600 employees with alleged communist and pro-*coup* activities. Most of those dismissed may have belonged to a communist controlled union before the *coup*, but that would probably have been about the extent of their 'crimes'. However, it was common knowledge at the time of their dismissal that Garuda was grossly overstaffed, and could not be made profitable without wholesale re-trenchments. And apart from widening the administration's 'credibility gap', such tactics obviously also help dull public awareness of real rather than imaginary

175

threats from communism, or any other kind of subversive activities.

Accordingly, without excluding the possibility of bizarre efforts on the part of the Communist Party remnants to create economic and political instability within the country, celebrated cases such as that of fifteen-year-old Purwati Prawirotrimo meet with a considerable degree of scepticism. In May 1969, Purwati was sentenced to seven years' imprisonment for her part in an alleged communist plot that provoked the Islamic population of Djatibarang, Indramaju, West Java, into burning the churches, schools and houses of local Christians. Purwati was supposed to have first attended a clandestine communist organized course in 'home economics' that, among others things, instructed pupils in the art of 'playing one group off against another'. Presumably after graduating with honours, she was assigned her subversive 'mission' in Djatibarang. After living with a Christian family for five months, she complained to a Muslim leader that she was being prevented from practising her Islamic faith, had been forced to eat pork and dog meat, and was being pressured into becoming a Christian. She did all this, she told the court, knowing that it would create trouble between the Islamic and Christian communities in Djatibarang. In another case, the especially depraved sexual behaviour of a mosque official in South Sumatra seemed at least to be explained to the court's satisfaction when police gave evidence that 'communist literature' had been found in the possession of the accused.

In exploiting the communist 'bogey', there is also a tendency to overlook the real causes of tension in regions such as Indramaju, Purwodadi and South Blitar. All are among what are called 'minus areas' in official Indonesian terminology – meaning that they suffer rice shortages. In an account of famine in the Indramaju area during October 1970, for instance, an Indonesian journalist estimated that from one-quarter to one-third of a population of about one million was on the verge of starvation. Purwodadi in Central Java is another notorious poverty-stricken area – a fact that was not normally stressed in official claims that the place had become a 'bastion for underground communist activities'. Similarly, South Blitar in East Java is among the most economically depressed regions in all Java. With a history of government neglect possibly without parallel, the region has long been recognized as the seat of a cult that glorified crime and violence, and consequently had attracted a motley collection of murderers and thieves. Only after military authorities learned that important communist leaders were hiding out in the area was any effort made to improve living conditions among the population of about 250,000.

And while many Indonesian leaders are generally aware that poverty rather than communism is their real enemy, the problem of translating this realization into tangible results still remains. When I visited South Blitar in May 1969, for instance, I was impressed by the programme of economic rehabilitation then under way. Hundreds of thousands of fruit-bearing trees had already been planted on some of the barren, impoverished hills to prevent further erosion. More than 4,000 houses had been moved into village settlements along some of 250 miles of roadway that was under repair. Thousands of householders had been encouraged to grow new crops, and the government had established village farms for seedlings and built tapioca mills, small iron founderies and tile factories, and even a small textile factory using handlooms. They had also erected new schools, health centres, mosques and market places. Although the problems the local people faced were obviously still staggering, much had been achieved in less than twelve months. But most Indonesians I spoke with feared that after the initial burst of activity, government interest would decline, and the region would quickly fall into neglect again.

There are, then, several aspects to the threat communism poses to political and economic stability in the post-*coup* period. It is unlikely that the remnants of the once-powerful Communist Party can regroup and re-organize themselves to present a real military danger in the foreseeable future. The Party has clearly suffered a crippling blow, and there are now divisions and rivalries within its ranks, including Moscow-oriented members as well as those pursuing the Peking line. The Party remnants also seem to be very much thrown on their own resources, and have enormous organizational, logistic and communication problems to overcome. Further, the South Blitar debacle appears to support Aidit's old argument that an armed struggle is not possible in overcrowded Java while the army holds an overwhelming monopoly of naked physical force. But this does not mean that communist insurgency cannot still make quite serious demands on the limited resources of the post-*coup* administration, as is already evident from events in Central and East Java and West Kalimantan.

However, the greatest danger appears to lie in the way the administration approaches the real problems of poverty and social injustice on which communism thrives. The Communist Party has always shown itself to be more genuinely concerned with the welfare of the rural people than either the military or other political party leaders. And today, more than ever before, the remnants of the Party are forced to share the peasants' unpleasant lot, perhaps hiding their true identity and biding their time. Thus if instead of eradicating the causes of communism, Indonesian leaders merely exploit the communist 'bogey' as a political weapon for striking down opponents and political rivals, justifying further repressive measures and injustices, and covering up their own shortcomings, then increased political and economic turbulence is inevitable, and communism will most probably rise again as Sudisman predicted.

Chapter 9

The Religious Problem

'In the interest of peace,' warned the brief message scrawled overnight upon the door of a newly built Methodist church, 'please move to another site as quickly as possible. Respect Islamic tolerance.' Their warning ignored, angry Muslims met, argued among themselves, then acted. Armed with anything they could lay their hands on, about 400 marched upon the church and wrecked it. They then turned upon another house used by the Methodists for prayer meetings, and, for good measure, ransacked the local Catholic church as well. Those events in April 1967 at Meulaboh, on the remote west coast of Atjeh (Sumatra), marked the beginnings of a series of violent clashes between Muslims and Christians in post-*coup* Indonesia. So volatile and potentially explosive had the situation become by the early seventies that a Jakarta daily declared in March 1970 only months before the ailing former President died: 'Sukarno used to say that without him, Indonesia would be torn apart by religious conflict. Let us prevent him from making a comeback as the only one who can save the nation from this present religious strife.'

The kind of struggle that could erupt has already been outlined by Islamic leaders. 'Islam is now being teased by the Catholic and Protestant faiths, which aim at kicking Islam out of Indonesia,' wrote one during September 1967. 'The sleeping giant of Islam already begins to feel disturbed and the time may come when it will completely awake and a "to be or not to be" struggle could ensue, which nobody dares even contemplate.' Less dramatically, but no less insistently, the former Prime Minister, Muhammad Natsir, told Muslim preachers in May 1969: 'Our Christian brothers maintain they were entrusted with the

179

sacred mission of spreading the gospel to the ends of the earth. For this mission, the Christians of Indonesia say they will do their best and are ready to sacrifice whatever they may possess. If such is the determination of Indonesian Christians, we Muslims also have a duty to preach Islamic doctrine to the Indonesian people, and we, too, are willing to sacrifice everything. Thus both Muslims and Christians are confident that they are carrying on sacred missions for which they could suffer martyrdom. If this is our point of departure, the problem between the Muslims and Christians is solved, especially if both sides are prepared to race for paradise through martyrdom . . .'

Few leaders, either Muslim or Christian, believe that bloodshed is the answer – and Natsir is certainly not among them. But the fanaticism that elements of both faiths have revealed in the past cannot help but cast a storm cloud over the prospects of their continued peaceful coexistence. In Atjeh, for instance, where the trouble began, many Muslims are still taught that death as a martyr in a 'Holy War' is easy and simple. '. . . to die in the Holy War is nothing,' runs the still popular epic used to urge young Muslims into battle against the Dutch during the nineteenth century. 'It is like being tickled till we fall and roll over (laughing) . . . Then comes a heavenly princess; she cradles you in her lap and wipes away the blood, her heart all yours . . .' In contrast, to die in any other way is to confront the 'Angel of Death' which is 'more terrible than being hacked by a sword . . . a thousand times.' Even after the Dutch finally subdued the Atjehnese people, a private form of 'Holy War' continued during the early twentieth century whereby young Atjehnese men sought a speedy passage to paradise by murdering an 'infidel' – in this case, usually a Dutch official. Since independence, much the same fanaticism has inspired extremist Muslim leaders like S. M. Kartosuwirjo, who led the *Darul Islam* (Islamic State) rebel movement in West Java from 1948 until his capture in June 1962, Daud Beureueh in Atjeh and Kahar Muzakar in South Sulawesi.

More recently, following the attempted *coup,* many Muslims joined the killings believing they were engaged in a 'Holy War' against communist 'infidels'.

Although numerically dominant, Muslims often view Christians with great distrust, and react swiftly to Christian provocations. Meulaboh, for instance, with a population of about 30,000, is almost 100 per cent Muslim. Of perhaps 200 Christians living there at the time of the outburst, only sixty to seventy were Methodists. Since forming an evangelical group in the town in 1962, they had met with continual harassment and frustration in their efforts to open a church, but this was most probably because they sought a prominent position in the town. They were forced to sell the first church they built in 1964 when Muslims protested over its nearness to a mosque. They bought another site, but this was taken from them after the *coup* by the new town administration and a further site offered in its place. And only after the church was nearly finished were they told the location was still unacceptable because many Muslim families lived nearby. At least, that is the Methodists' side of the story. The Muslims claim they did not know that a church was being built on the site. They also indicate that had the church been built on the outskirts of the town, no trouble would have occurred.

Other incidents since the 'Meulaboh affair' also highlight Christian provocations and Muslim sensitivity. In the South Sulawesi provincial capital of Makassar early in October 1967, rioting Muslims damaged about twenty Christian churches and schools because a Christian teacher had allegedly insulted the prophet Muhammad. According to Muslims, the trouble could have been averted if Christian leaders had been prepared to make a retraction and condemn the teacher's behaviour – but this, apparently, they were not prepared to do. Other lesser incidents followed with reports of a hand-grenade being thrown into a Catholic church in Surabaja, East Java, attempts to set fire to two churches at Seribu Laksa village in North

181

Sumatra, and a mosque being damaged by fire in Padang Bulan, North Sumatra. The episode in Djatibarang, West Java, in January 1968, mentioned in the previous chapter (p. 176), however, involved quite extensive damage to Christian churches, schools and houses.

In Central and East Java, numerous clashes also flared between Muslims and Christians, but many went unreported as both government officials and responsible religious leaders made every effort to avoid further inflaming the issue. But late in April 1969, Jakarta had its own 'Meulaboh affair' in the suburb of Slipi when about 500 Muslims ransacked a newly built Protestant church in a predominantly Muslim area. And one influential Muslim paper, commenting on the incident, declared: 'Affairs like that in Slipi will repeat themselves again and again as long as the international Christian missions continue to employ their abundant financial resources to destroy the potentialities of the Indonesian Muslim majority. As long as the current Christianization aimed directly at Indonesian Muslims is not prevented and prohibited by the government, Indonesian Muslims will grow more and more restless and resentful.'

The financial plight of the Muslims compared with the Christians was one of several grievances brought forward during the public debate sparked off by the Meulaboh and Makassar incidents. In parliament in July 1967, Muslim interests attempted to have the government control the flow of all foreign aid for missionary purposes, including funds, materials and foreign missionaries. They also sought restrictions on the activities of Christian missionaries which were clearly directed at preventing changes in the established 'balance' between Muslims and Christians in the country. Articles in Muslim publications carried allegations that Christian missionaries were exploiting all kinds of tricks – including interest free loans – to win over converts. In South Sumarta, one article alleged, missionaries had built hospitals and health clinics in Muslim strongholds, and were offering free medical treatment to entice Muslims into becoming Christians.

They were also supposed to be 'bribing' Muslims into helping build Christian churches with gifts of foodstuffs, textiles and cigarettes, offering big discounts on the hire of tractors for farmers who attended their churches, and helping churchgoers buy livestock on easy terms. As a result, the article claimed, Muslim villagers were joining Christian churches by the 'hundreds and thousands'.

Muslim accusations also highlighted the superior organization of the missionary activities of the Christian minorities. In an outspoken, dramatic comment that generally reflected the widespread feeling among even more moderate elements of Muslim society, one Muslim leader wrote: 'With one "field marshal" (cardinal) and twenty-one "generals" (bishops), the Catholics are already strong enough to launch a large-scale spiritual invasion against the weak impoverished Indonesian people. The Indonesian Council of Churches, under the leadership of former Lieutenant General Simatupang, has minutely planned its programme for the next ten to twenty years, whereby, at some time in the future, Islam will be kicked out into the Indonesian Ocean (as Sukarno renamed the Indian Ocean). The Council of Churches divides Indonesia into various regions, and its work programme is not based on tolerance and coexistence with Islam. No, its programme is to Christianize the Muslims – to Christianize the whole of Indonesia. If Muslims are expected to respond to this situation with slogans such as "tolerance, democracy, religious freedom, basic human rights" and so on, it is not reasonable.'

For their part, the Christian minorities are equally adamant that incidents such as had occurred at Meulaboh were a direct violation of religious freedom guaranteed under the Indonesian Constitution and expressed in the state philosophy *Pantja Sila* (p. 43). They were quick to quote article 29 of the Constitution which states:

(1) The State shall be based upon Belief in the One, Supreme God.

(2) The State shall guarantee freedom to every resident

to adhere to his respective religion and to perform his religious duties in conformity with that religion and that faith.

They also pointed out that the first principle of *Pantja Sila*, Belief in the One Supreme God, was intended to safeguard the right of every Indonesian to believe in his own God. (The Makassar incident had occurred on 1 October, which since the *coup* had been celebrated as '*Pantja Sila* Day'.) They argued that when Sukarno had enunciated the *Pantja Sila* in June 1945, he had said: 'The Christian should worship God according to the teachings of Jesus Christ, Muslims according to the teachings of the Prophet Muhammad, Buddhists should perform their religious ceremonies in accordance with the books they have. But let us all believe in God . . .'

In an effort to prevent major conflict from erupting, the administration sponsored discussions between all religious groups late in 1967. Opening the meeting, Suharto reaffirmed the basic guarantees for religious freedom under the Constitution and the *Pantja Sila*. He also agreed that all religions had the right to disseminate their teachings, though without resorting to force. But he opened the way for a possible freezing of the existing balance between the various faiths in Indonesia by declaring that the 'government should be cautious of religious activities aimed merely at increasing the numbers of followers, especially when it seemed to one religion that these efforts were merely aimed at attracting its own followers.' Out of this arose the proposal pressed by Muslims that missionary activities should be banned among people already professing a religion, and that each religion should concentrate on improving the 'quality' of its followers rather than the 'quantity'. This the Christian religions categorically rejected, much to Suharto's early anger. But he later accepted their argument that the proposal, in fact, was identical with the spirit, if not the letter, of the 'Jakarta Charter' which many Indonesians, both Christians and non-Christians, have opposed since the struggle for independence began.

With the emergence of the 'Jakarta Charter' as an issue, the fuller political dimensions of the dispute came more clearly into view. The 'Jakarta Charter', drawn up in 1945, affirms not merely that the Republic of Indonesia should have 'belief in God' as one of its bases, but that there should be 'the obligation of practising the laws of Islam for the adherents of that religion, in accordance with the principles of just and civilized humanity'. These were the minimal demands Muslims sought during the debate between those favouring an Islamic state and those wanting a secular national state prior to the proclamation of the Republic. They failed to get the 'Jakarta Charter' incorporated into the body of the Constitution, but have not given up hope that its sentiments may eventually gain the weight of state law. In the late fifties, for example, during the transition from parliamentary democracy to Guided Democracy, Muslims tried to have the Constitution amended but failed to muster the necessary two-thirds majority.

Christians alone could never have prevented the establishment of an Islamic state in Indonesia – and this is the crucial point of the political issue. At no time have Christians ever numbered more than six or seven per cent of the population. Less than another three per cent are Hindu or Buddhist (though since the *coup* increasing numbers have been turning to these religions), and the remainder – about ninety per cent – are usually considered Muslims. But as already mentioned in Chapter 2 (pp. 53-4), the Islamization of Indonesia was 'never actually fully consummated'. Among both the aristocracy and peasantry of Central and East Java especially, the 'statistical' or nominal Muslim emerged. For the most part, these are Muslims only on about four occasions during their lives – at their birth, circumcision, marriage and death. They may attend prayers at the mosque, but their hearts still belong to the richly imaginative deities and ancestoral figures of their ancient beliefs and mythology. Nor can they completely snap the bonds of traditional customs that are intimately interwoven with those beliefs and regulate much of their lives. Only in isolated pockets of Indonesia – such as the province of Atjeh and parts of West Sumatra – has traditional village *adat* been effectively dominated by Islam.

Thus Islam does not have a political majority in Indonesia despite the nominal allegiance of about 90 per cent of the population. A more realistic indication of its real political strength can be found in the 1955 general election results when Muslim political parties captured about forty-three per cent of the total vote. But Sukarno seriously curtailed the political voice of Islam when he banned the largest Muslim party, the Masjumi (which accounted for nearly half the Muslim vote), in 1960 for its involvement in the rebellions of the late fifties.

In the view of many Muslims, the banning of the Masjumi was further proof of a 'conspiracy' to keep Islam politically weak in Indonesia. Since independence, Islam allegedly has been under constant attack. When I interviewed Daud Beureueh in March 1960, for instance, he was still adamant that Islam would have emerged with a majority had elections been held promptly after the victory over the Dutch. He insisted that the main reason elections were delayed until 1955 was so that the nationalist and communist forces could be strengthened, and the Muslims weakened. He especially blamed Sukarno, and his formulation of *Pantja Sila*, for the failure of Islam to gain the political ascendancy.

While there may be some truth in these arguments, many of the weaknesses and failings of Islam arise from within its own ranks. Originally united as the Masjumi – fragile as the unity undoubtedly was – Muslims had split into four political parties well before the 1955 elections: the Masjumi, the Religious Scholars League (NU), the Islamic Association Party of Indonesia (PSII), and the Islamic Education Movement (Perti). Personal ambitions and rivalries among Muslim leaders played a major role in the formation of each party, and factions within each party further impaired Muslim strength. But the divisions were reinforced by conflicting views of Islam, as well as ethnic and other differences. Of the two major parties, the Masjumi and the Religious Scholars League, the former generally represented the more progressive, modern-oriented Islam of the Outer Islands and West Java, while the latter found its strength in the conservative, corrupted Islam of the rural regions of Central and East Java. And it was the leaders of the Religious Scholars League, who were most ready to compromise with Sukarno, and must share responsibility for the banning of Masjumi in 1960.

*

Although frustrated during the fifties and early sixties, Muslim parties fully expected their political stocks to rise during the post-*coup* period since they had played a major role in crushing the Communist Party. The Masjumi, especially, hoped for speedy rehabilitation in the anti-communist, anti-Sukarno climate that the *coup* and the failure of Guided Democracy had encouraged. With the Communist Party no longer a dominating faction in Indonesian politics, Muslims not only confidently looked forward to attaining a political majority, but also to the wider practices of an Islamic way of life throughout the country, if not the actual attainment of an Islamic state.

Their expectations quickly proved mistaken. Far from welcoming a close alliance with Muslim power, the army chose to keep the Muslims at 'arms length' – and this was a reflection of the strong position of ethnic Javanese forces within the officer corps. Firmly refusing to revoke the ban on the Masjumi party, Suharto also showed that while he wanted to give former Masjumi voters a political voice, he did not want the old Masjumi leaders dominating post-*coup* Indonesian politics. Only after lengthy negotiations did he approve the formation in February 1968 of a new Muslim party, called the Indonesian Muslim Party (Parmusi, or PMI), on the express condition that its executive body should exclude former Masjumi leaders. And when in November 1968, the Muslim Party tried to reinstate some of these figures, the government blocked their appointment. Behind the scenes, former Masjumi leaders such as Prawoto Mangkusasmito, Burhanuddin Harahap, Muhammad Natsir and Muhammad Roem, were clearly playing an active role, but the government continued to frustrate their efforts to consolidate, and helped split the party's leadership again in 1970. As a result, some Muslim leaders were threatening that '12 million Muslims' might boycott the July 1971 national elections.

Other developments exacerbated Muslim disappointment. Despite the close links the Nationalist Party had established both with Sukarno and the Communist Party, it soon became apparent that the army wanted the party 'rehabilitated' and strengthened as a counter-weight to Muslim power. At the same time, it seemed the army was intent on maintaining disunity among Muslim groups. During the early part of 1969, for instance, the army repeatedly frustrated the efforts of Muslim parties to get together and try to settle their differences. In addition, important posts in both the government and the army were being filled by non-Muslims. As his successor to the army command, Suharto promoted a Protestant, General Maraden Panggabean. And the leader of the Catholic Party (which polled only two per cent of the votes in the 1955 elections), Frans Seda, outranked Muslim leaders in the cabinet, first as Minister of Finance until Muslim pressure forced his removal from that portfolio in mid-1968, and then as Minister of Communications. Through their excellent organization and contacts in 'high places', the Catholics especially were seen by the Muslims as exerting an undue influence on government affairs. Further, although Suharto kept the ex-Masjumi leaders in political quarantine, he appointed another rebel leader, the economist Dr Sumitro Djojohadikusumo, to his cabinet in mid-1968.

But possibly the most alarming post-*coup* development

for many Muslim leaders was the dramatic expansion of the Christian churches. After decades of either disappointing or unspectacular growth, the Christian churches suddenly found hundreds of thousands of people clamouring at their doors. Far from needing to seek converts, most found they could not cope with the demand. Undoubtedly this phenomenon was closely related to the traumatic effects of the post-*coup* blood-letting and the army purge against the Communist Party. Membership in a non-communist body or organization often provided security against possible arrest as a suspected communist. Consequently, the sincerity of many of the would-be converts was probably open to question, and most churches viewed them with considerable caution. But what apparently caused consternation among many Muslim leaders was that so many people should prefer to seek membership in Christian churches (and especially too among Hindu and Buddhist religions in Central and East Java) rather than embrace the Muslim faith.

*

Even so, the actions of some Muslim leaders during the post-*coup* period scarcely helped their overall cause. In Atjeh, for instance, where Meulaboh provided the first case of any civil or military administration giving way to Muslim pressure, it is difficult to see how Christians were in any way a threat to Muslim supremacy. Except for about 3,000 Christians, the entire population of more than two million in the province profess Islam. Yet following the Meulaboh incident many Muslim leaders agitated for the closing of all Christian churches in the province. At Pulau Banjak, islands near the west coast, conditions were made so intolerable for Christians that several hundred fled to the more remote Nias islands in mid-1968. And in many parts of the province, Christians were subjected to continual public harassment and abuse. During a visit to Atjeh in March 1969, I found that the only Catholic priest in the province was a virtual prisoner in

189

his church in the provincial capital of Banda Atjeh. He was not prohibited from travelling, but feared that doing so might be regarded as 'provocative behaviour'. Already the army had narrowly prevented one attempt by Muslim groups to destroy his church, and he was determined not to give them the slightest excuse for making another attempt.

Nor were Christians the only target of Muslim agitation in Atjeh. Communists, Chinese, members of the Nationalist Party, non-Atjehnese – all felt the wrath of Islam during the post-*coup* period. The Atjehnese were among the first to begin the blood-letting that followed the *coup*. Extending the purge to the Chinese population – since many were communists, or identified with communism, and non-Muslim – they forced about 7,000 Chinese holding Peking passports to flee the province leaving most of their possessions behind, and persuaded another 4,000 with Indonesian citizenship to acquire Indonesian names and embrace Islam. They also dealt swiftly with members of the Nationalist Party in the region, forcing them to 'voluntarily' disband their organization. (In 1970, under central government pressure, the Party was allowed to recommence its activities, but demonstrators threw stones during an official reopening ceremony attended by a cabinet minister from Jakarta.) And, late in 1968, the provincial legislature defied the central government in enacting a bill imposing Islamic law on all followers of Islam in the province.

Behind these moves were the *Ulama* – the powerful scholars and teachers of Islam, such as Daud Beureueh. During 1966, with the establishment of the Council of *Ulama*, they gained institutional standing within the provincial government. Although the full council of all *Ulama* throughout the province meets only once a year, a working body of fifty members meets when necessary. While officially the council is only an advisory body with the task of assisting the region 'co-ordinate and direct the potentials of the Muslim people for the development of the region', its authority is such that its 'advice' can scarcely be ignored. Nor does its role end with 'advice'. Referring to the controversial move enacting Islamic law in the province, the secretary of the council told me in 1969 that the council would retain a 'guiding role' over the implementation of the law by the provincial administration.

It is precisely the kind of situation that has developed in Atjeh since the *coup* that causes the army not to be well disposed towards Muslim groups. Many army leaders fear that the Muslim parties pay only lip-service to the *Pantja Sila* – which asserts the equal importance of the five principles of belief in One God, Nationalism, Internationalism, Democracy and Social Justice – and, that given the opportunity, would impose Islamic law throughout Indonesia. They argue that together with the communists, radical Muslim elements have been the principal exponents of armed rebellion against central government authority since the formation of the Republic. They note that leaders such as Beureueh are openly critical of the *Pantja Sila*, asserting that only Islam can effectively unite Indonesia. They also argue that while Muslim parties may not publicly advocate an Islamic state, they all support developments in Atjeh since the *coup* which bear an unmistakable trend towards the establishment of an Islamic state. And they are concerned that other strongly Muslim regions, such as West Sumatra, South Sumatra, South Kalimantan and South Sulawesi, should attempt to follow Atjeh's example. In fact, Kendari in South Sulawesi did make such an attempt, but the central government was able to block, and reverse, the move.

In justifying developments in Atjeh, Muslims argue that Islamic laws have been a 'way of life' for the Atjehnese for several hundred years. As a result, they have become indistinguishable from traditional customs (*adat*). And since the central government encourages the implementation of traditional laws in the regions, it should not object to the imposition of Islamic law in Atjeh. A former governor of Atjeh, Ali Hasjmy, who lectures at the province's Islamic University, told me: 'Jakarta must understand the feelings of the people here. We have no intention of establishing an Islamic state and separating from Jakarta. We only want Islamic law valid in our everyday lives.'

Such arguments tend to gloss over the fact that Islam has been largely responsible for the atrophy of traditional custom in the province. The unrelenting attacks of Muslim leaders on the Uleebelang, the traditional rulers in the region, have played a major role in establishing the supremacy of Islam. Daud Beureueh and his followers delivered the final blow to the Uleebelang when they either murdered or drove them from the province immediately following the proclamation of independence. Whatever the shortcomings of the Uleebelang, the ruthlessness with which they were dealt with could scarcely have avoided causing some uneasiness among many Indonesians in other parts of the archipelago, and notably in Central and East Java. Likewise, if Baduis legend has any basis, it was the aggressiveness of Islam in the sixteenth century that largely caused the ancestors of Girang Adjal (pp. 37-40) to flee the court of King Suria Kantjana (who ruled over the kingdom of Padjadjaran in western Java) and seek refuge among the mountains.

The Javanese especially are not anxious that their traditional culture should suffer a similar fate. The 'statistical Muslims' of Central and East Java have reached an acceptable accommodation with the mystical, corrupted form of Islam that spread through Java during the fifteenth and sixteenth centuries. Even so, they remain wary of the second 'wave' of Islam – inspired by reformist Egyptian scholars – that aims at 'purifying' Islam, and which won widespread acceptance in the Outer Islands during the nineteenth and twentieth centuries, but so far has met with little success among rural Javanese. Since about three-quarters of the army officer corps is Javanese – and among them, the majority of those professing Islam would be 'statistical' Muslims – ethnic and cultural considerations clearly help explain why the army leadership is generally wary of Islam, and particularly of those Muslim leaders, such as the former Masjumi figures, who are identified with modern Islam.

This conflict between traditional authority and culture and Islam also underlies divisions within the ranks of Islam. The former Masjumi and the non-political Muslim organization, the Muhammadijah, are more generally identified with the 'reformed' Islam, and have found their strongest support in the regions outside Central and East Java. On the other hand, the Religious Scholars League (NU) is strongest in those regions, and is more closely identified with early Islam. Perti, a small party limited mainly to parts of Sumatra, including the remoter regions of west Atjeh, is also linked with the remnants of the mystical, corrupted Islam in those regions.

Islam is further divided between its conservative and progressive elements, and this often partly accounts for divisions within the various parties. During the early fifties, for example, the moderate, progressive elements joined with like-minded elements among the Nationalist Party to repress conservative, radical Muslim leaders such as Daud Beureueh in Atjeh. Beureueh, for instance, alleges that the Masjumi-Nationalist Party based government led by the moderate Masjumi leader, Dr Sukiman Wirjosandjojo, arrested about half of his top forty leaders in 1951 on the pretext that they were communists. In contrast with Beureueh, who has had little or no contact with Western thought, Sukiman and other prominent Muslim leaders such as Muhammad Natsir, were convinced that Muslims must come to terms with the West and take full advantage of the advances of Western science and technology. However, even Sukiman and Natsir differed in their views, and drew their support from conflicting elements of Indonesian society.

With the post-*coup* stress on economic development and 'modernization', Islam has come under renewed scrutiny for its apparent inability to confront the demands of the twentieth century in Indonesia. Its critics argue that the basic grievances many Muslims voice – that their ranks include the poorest and least privileged elements of Indonesian society, and that they are slipping further and further behind – are at least partly the consequences of the failure of Islam itself to adapt to the demands of the times. They point out that all too often the first concern of Muslim leaders is to build bigger and more impressive mosques, rather than show concern for the material backwardness and low level of education among many of their followers. They argue that this attitude stems largely from the fears of conservative Muslim leaders that modernization will weaken their hold and authority over the people by strengthening secular forces within society.

Some Muslim leaders appear to fear not only the possible erosion of religious values under the impact of modernization, but also rising demands for a more clear-cut separation between religious and state affairs. Addressing Muslim teachers in June 1970, the Minister of Religion, Kijaji Hadji Dachlan, took an unequivocal stand which generally reflected the widespread sentiment among Muslims. Defining modernization as the establishment of new institutions, concepts, views and values demanded by advances in science and technology, he declared it was acceptable only as long as it involved 'no changes in matters of faith and religious duties', since these 'cannot be modernized or altered according to man's wishes and opinions'. Muslims also vigorously press for greater, rather than less, government responsibility in religious matters, asserting: 'The state must be responsible for the religious development and performance of religious teachings in the life of the individual, of society, and the nation. If not, we will only repeat the disaster which has befallen, or will befall, the secular world, the West (capitalism), as well as the East (communism).'

Other Indonesians are equally concerned about the failure of Islam to move into the twentieth century – and especially the conservatism and narrow-mindedness of

Islam in Indonesia. Professor Takdir Alisjahbana, a prominent writer and thinker, claims that 'in philosophical development alone, Muslims are three to four centuries behind their colleagues in other groups.' Lieutenant General Mokoginta, a former Indonesian Ambassador to the United Arab Republic, has also publicly chided his fellow Muslim countrymen for their conservatism, puritanism and orthodoxy. 'Muslims in Indonesia think that modern trends and currents in cultural and social life are against Islam,' he notes. 'They also confuse everything Arab with Islam, so they visualize Arab society, even today, as to be even more conservative, puritan and orthodox because Islam came from that region. But Cairo is a modern city with theatres, casinos, cinemas – and even the well-known "belly dancers". In some Indonesian communities, it's considered appropriately "Islamic" for women, especially young girls and unmarried women, to go veiled "because it's like Arab women", which is completely untrue. Arab girls and women go unveiled and wear modern fashions, including the mini-skirt.' And a more progressive Jakarta Muslim daily in March 1970 lamented: 'While the few modern Muslim intellectuals have been preoccupied with politics, the traditional Muslims have been busy quarrelling about the permissibility of drinking beer, the date of Idulfitri (the end of the fasting month), religious films, and the like.'

But Christians must also share the blame for the religious tensions that have arisen. Their comparative prominence in government and national affairs is largely due to better educational opportunities offered through the activities of Christian missionaries in the country, both in the present and past. 'As a result, far too many Christians tend to look down on Muslims,' the leader of the Catholic Party, Frans Seda, admits. 'It's high time we started practising some of the Christian virtues we preach.' He believes a similar problem still exists among the different Christian churches. 'There is far too much animosity. These animosities were imported from Western

Europe along with the religions so that you had Catholics despising Protestants and Protestants also taking the attitude that "better the devil than Rome". Today, things are improving. There is a much better relationship, but we can do a lot more. We can also do much to improve the relationship between Christians and Muslims. The basic problem is that there is far too much mistrust and fear among Christians as well as Muslims. Christians are afraid of losing freedom of movement and rights. Muslims are afraid of losing ground. But we cannot build a wall around ourselves and live in isolation. It would be a backward step to create "religious pockets", or "tribes" based on religion.'

Unless greater understanding and co-operation can be fostered among Muslims and Christians, the 'religious issue' will remain potentially explosive. One of the tragedies of the early post-*coup* conflict was the way it damaged previous harmonious relations in some parts of the archipelago, such as the Moluccas and North Sulawesi. There are indications that Christians are now accepting greater responsibility for helping improve the living conditions of all Indonesians, irrespective of their religious beliefs. But until the 'gap' between the social position of Muslims and Christians can be narrowed significantly, and Muslims assume a greater responsibility in national affairs, a major threat to the unity and welfare of the entire nation remains. 'What we are dealing with is the destiny and survival of the state we jointly established and love,' says Muhammad Natsir. 'The problem is, can we, the citizens of the Republic of Indonesia, both Muslims and Christians, create a *modus vivendi* for peaceful coexistence and mutual respect for each other's identity.' It is a cry from the heart – but only in the future will the answer become known.

Chapter 10

Continuity *versus* Change

At the funeral of Rene Louis Coenraad, students publicly likened the repression of civilians in Indonesia to the lot of American Negroes. Coenraad, a young engineering student at the Bandung Institute of Technology died early in October 1970, allegedly shot by a cadet from the Sukabumi Police Academy during a brawl after a stormy soccer game between the technology students and the police cadets. His funeral over, hundreds of students drove through the streets of Jakarta hurling insults at the military and brandishing placards that proclaimed the military were killers of the people rather than their protectors. In their daily newspaper, *Harian KAMI*, the students continued their tirade against the military in stinging editorials under headings such as 'Have gun will terrorize . . . '. They declared that the shot that killed Coenraad had begun a new student movement – the civil rights movement. 'What must be settled is not just the incident,' they argued, 'but more especially its cause: the habit of arbitrariness produced by the unbalanced relations between the military and civilians.'

Although many Indonesians may not have a great love for their military, the students' call for a popular 'civil rights' movement was less than an outstanding success. Far from persuading the public that another national martyr had been born, they may even have further antagonized many people. For some Indonesians apparently took the view that Coenraad's death was another tragic incident that could easily have been avoided had the students been better behaved, and their sympathies were probably more with the police cadets.

Coenraad's death had climaxed several months of growing

197

ill-feeling between some of the technology students and the police cadets. As part of their training, the cadets were given certain duties on occasions, such as providing security at sporting functions and clearing Bandung of tramps and prostitutes on the eve of important conferences. At times, they had also extended their activities to taking action against youths with long hair and Western style of dress, and this especially had brought them into conflict with some of the students. In retaliation, these wore wigs and brandished imitation scissors as they jeered and hooted the cadets from the sidelines during the soccer game. And when one cadet among the spectators lost his police cap, it was quickly tossed about among the students and trampled upon. In one of the brawls that followed, Coenraad was killed. Later, ignoring accepted protocol, about 500 students descended on Jakarta, demanding an immediate audience with President Suharto to seek redress for Coenraad's death.

By their behaviour, and the reaction they met, the students again highlighted the deep-seated conflict between traditional forces and those pressing for fundamental social change in 20th century Indonesia. It was this kind of behaviour that had largely led to the rupture of the early army-student alliance during the campaign to remove Sukarno from power (pp. 99-100). And it had possibly reached new heights during the 1970 outcry against corruption when the students were frequently criticized for lacking 'Eastern good manners'. For the students flouted traditionally accepted codes of behaviour in pressing their demands, and the 'civil rights' they sought were more readily equated with Western than Eastern attitudes towards authority and the place of the individual in society.

Without digging too deeply into what is a highly complex issue, this cultural 'gap' involves a wide range of issues in Indonesia today. The students, and other Indonesians who hold similar views, echo the lament of the Dutch-educated Indonesian socialist leader Sutan Sjahrir who realized that he had been 'too abstract' for his people

– too far removed from 'the framework of their concepts, too "Western". They have been, for me, too inert.' Sjahrir tried to breathe some of the West's life and vigour into the passive Eastern spirit of his people. 'For me,' he wrote, [despite its brutality and its coarseness] 'the West signifies forceful, dynamic, and active life. It is a sort of Faust that I admire, and I am convinced that only by a utilization of this dynamism of the West can the East be released from its slavery and subjugation.' But it was Sukarno – fossicking among the 'buried treasure' of the past – who won the applause and approval of most Indonesian people.

Among those sections of the Indonesian press supporting the students, this cultural conflict is clearly recognized. At the death of Coenraad, for instance, Mochtar Lubis's *Indonesia Raya*, outspokenly condemned the young student's 'murder' as 'only one instance in the long sequence of violations of values in this country', and a 'symptom of the sickness of our society's mentality'. The paper added:

Since the honeymoon of the armed forces-student 'partnership' in the struggle to topple the regime of Sukarno and the Communist Party, the hopes of the younger people have been replaced by disappointment after disappointment. They thought that with Sukarno's fall and the Communist Party's destruction, there would be fundamental reforms in their country. They witnessed a change of people but they have been waiting in vain for a change in the structure of government and state institutions. They have been waiting in vain for improvements in the world of education. They have noticed with frustration how the armed forces are moving farther and farther away from them. They are alarmed about their future. Rene Coenraad's murder was the spark that blew up the suppressed disappointment and frustration . . . [1]

In an earlier editorial, *Indonesia Raya* had also noted

1. *Indonesia Raya*, Jakarta, 15 October 1970.

that Coenraad's death should not be blamed upon the armed forces, or police alone: 'Those who apply force to solve problems are not confined to the armed forces,' the paper continued. 'Also among civilians, there are many people of a like attitude.'

Later the same month Coenraad died, the intensity of the conflict was even more clearly exposed by a split within the ranks of the Indonesian press. Following a stormy annual meeting, the Indonesian Journalists' Association (PWI) emerged with two competing executive bodies. One was led by B. M. Diah, a former Minister of Information in Suharto's early cabinet, and the founder and publisher of *Merdeka*; the other by Rosihan Anwar, a leading political commentator and editor of *Pedoman*. It is difficult to generalize, but the two groups represented differing attitudes towards traditional and foreign (especially Western) values within society and the kinds of changes and policies needed to modernize and bring about economic development in Indonesia.

Some of the areas of disagreement between the two factions were evident from the sharp exchange that followed the split. The Diah faction depicted its opponents as a 'dangerous minority', who behind 'their slogans of rule of law, basic human rights, solidarity, purity of profession and democracy', tried to impose their will upon the majority. Far from being 'something real that is rooted in Indonesian society', they were little more than a 'handful of people' who wanted to be used as 'pack horses' for alien influences. The Anwar faction asserted that Diah and his supporters were 'neo-feudalists', 'opportunists' and 'Sukarnoists'. Far from practising 'real journalism', they merely excelled in the 'thoughtless repetition' of government statements.

But the most significant aspect of the dispute was the government's own clumsy involvement. Apparently, before the journalists met, certain military and civilian officials had mapped out a strategy whereby they were confident Diah would win the election. But Rosihan Anwar upset their calculations by making a late nomination. His personal prestige narrowly swung the vote against Diah and his supporters, who then protested that the association's rules and voting procedures were undemocratic. Not to be thwarted, these elements reconvened and named Diah's rival executive. And lest there be any doubt about his official 'sponsorship', government controlled news media in Jakarta blacked out all news of the Anwar executive, and the Minister of Information, Budiardjo, promptly recognized the PWI under the Diah executive.

By its involvement, the government highlighted both its growing impatience with those demanding reform as well as its essentially conservative, traditional Javanese bias. The vigour and style of the anti-corruption campaign during 1970 had especially caused great irritation and annoyance among elements of the administration, including Suharto. At the height of the campaign in mid-1970, Suharto contrasted the demonstrators' noisy agitation with the atmosphere of calm he found prevailing in the rural regions of Java. Indonesia, he reminded the students, ironically using an argument Sukarno favoured during the campaign to remove him from power, did not merely consist of cities like Jakarta, Bandung and other major centres, but also tens of thousands of villages.

Early in 1970, the students were also pointedly reminded by the military of a traditional Javanese form of protest called *pépé* – meaning 'being out in the sun'. Anyone with a gripe against the government, dressed in white and sat patiently with head bowed in front of the king's palace from early morning until late in the day. On learning of the presence of a *pépé*, the king would call him in, listen to his complaint, and then order whatever action he thought appropriate. 'Demonstrations', the military warned, 'are good as instruments of democracy only as long as they are "proper" and under control.'

In view of the predominant Javanese influence in the government, its reaction was not particularly surprising. Compared with customary Eastern courtesy, both the students' behaviour and the support and encouragement they received from papers generally identified with the Anwar faction had often been extremely provocative (as was also the case during Sukarno's overthrow). For example, when the Wilopo commission investigating corruption reported that the Attorney General's department should be more energetic in dealing with corruption, students presented the Attorney General, Major General Sugih Arto, with a box of medicines that reportedly included aphrodisiac and a tonic for pregnant women.

Later the same month, the students also tried to present the Attorney General with a mock award as a 'national hero' and 'meritorious fighter for the eradication of corruption' in recognition of prosecutions against nine minor public servants. Each was charged with corruption involving sums ranging from less than $100 to, in one instance, about 40 cents. Angrily Sugih Arto turned his back on the students, deploring their behaviour as 'against Oriental good manners'. Similarly, Suharto could barely conceal his anger when receiving the leader of a students' delegation from Jogjakarta, Central Java, who made a great show of affecting Javanese courtesy in approaching him to present a petition against corruption. Glancing at the signatories to the petition, Suharto commented that there were no Javanese names among them (although the students concerned were studying in Jogjakarta, they were all from other parts of Indonesia), and added that they would do well to learn both the spirit as well as the form of Javanese custom.

The students' disrespectful behaviour contrasts sharply with the lessons traditional Javanese shadow theatre (*wajang*) still stresses. Among persons whose advice should always be followed are firstly, parents (father and mother); secondly, teachers (including prophets); and thirdly, the authorities (state officials). Even when any of these people are clearly in the wrong, they are still entitled to complete respect and courtesy. Accordingly, students argue: 'It was accidental but fortunate that few Javanese students were in the vanguard of the KAMI-KAPPI action fronts in late 1965 and 1966. Otherwise, the actions would have been hampered and obstructed by this feudal attitude.'

During the mid-1970 anti-corruption campaign, the attitude of both the students and certain elements of the press supporting them apparently provoked Suharto into threatening to take action against some papers. 'If newspapers like *Indonesia Raya* and *Nusantara* (published by a wealthy Muslim businessman) continue to make trouble, they will be dealt with firmly', the Nationalist Party paper, *Suluh Marhaen*, quoted Suharto as telling one gathering of students. Approvingly, *Suluh Marhaen* commented:

we condemn every action to curb the press. But in the case the President referred to, we understand the problem fully. If people wish to practise the freedom of the press as prevails in Western countries, the Indonesian people who are imbued with *Pantja Sila* values will object . . . [1]

And following the split in the Indonesian Journalists' Association, *Suluh Marhaen* intensified its attacks on *Nusantara*, caustically asserting that the paper 'appears daily with its Westernized critical stand – a hocus-pocus of chatter and high-sounding foreign-Dutch phrases – (and) is not in tune with the people who under present circumstances object to its kind of high à la liberalism journalism'.

*

In the view of some Indonesians, therefore, the trend established by government intervention in political affairs since the 1965 *coup* evokes disturbing echoes of the past, and foreshadows a gloomy future for democracy and the right to dissent in Indonesia during the seventies. By strengthening traditional Javanese social and political forces and persistently blocking the growth of the more

1. *Suluh Marhaen*, Jakarta, 5 August 1970.

modern, Western-oriented, non-Javanese elements of society, the military has increasingly shown a distinct preference for the kind of authoritarian, paternalistic pattern of rule Sukarno favoured under Guided Democracy. Figures like Hadisubeno, whose election as chairman of the Nationalist Party (PNI) the government had aided in April 1970 (see p. 134), and Diah in the Indonesian Journalists' Association dispute, were noted for their great admiration for Sukarno and his teachings, though both had fallen out with him on the question of the Communist Party. Despite an official ban on Sukarno's teachings, Diah's *Merdeka* even declared in the heat of the debate over the journalists' split in October 1970 that 'Sukarnoism' had been the 'guiding principle' of the paper's struggle 'in the past, now and in the future'.

At the same time, this only underlines the broad division existing within Indonesian society on the question of democracy, largely as a consequence of the cultural conflict. On the one hand, democracy is defined in the traditional Javanese terms of *mupakat* (agreement) and *musjawarat* (consultations or discussion), and seen in vague, emotional terms as an abstract symbol of future aspirations and equated with the 'just and prosperous society' that all desire, or as a legitimizing principle and an educational and nation-building force. On the other hand, democracy is also seen – especially among the more Western-oriented, non-Javanese who feel overwhelmed by Javanese dominance – as a liberating force, freeing people from the shackles of traditional authoritarian tendencies, and allowing them to develop their individual personalities and talents. In this sense, the stress falls more on the idea of institutional checks on authoritarian and autocratic tendencies, on the need for countervailing power, checks and balances, and on individual rights, minority rights, rule of law and institutionalized opposition.

As already mentioned, the democracy Sukarno championed found its roots in the idealized version of simple village life. It was the 'rediscovery of the treasury of the

Indonesian people which has lain buried during hundreds of years of foreign rule'. Through *musjawarat* (discussion), the village people reached *mupakat* (agreement) without contests between opposing views, or resolutions and counter-resolutions which might be forced through by a majority of votes, but through a persistent effort to find common ground in solving a problem. Sukarno called this the democracy of 'jointly formulating the truth'. At other times, he likened it to the 'democracy of the family system'. And few Indonesians have critically examined his assertions, especially to inquire as to whether the system is really suitable for building a modern nation-state from such a diverse people. But an American scholar, Donald Weatherbee, has less flatteringly likened the system to 'primitive democracy' or 'primitive totalitarianism'.

Sukarno himself readily acknowledged the authoritarian aspects of traditional Indonesian democracy. The key ingredient was 'guidance'. To the 'guider' fell the task of reconciling conflicting views into a formulation 'palatable to each faction'. Without strong leadership capable of synthesizing the final decision, the system failed, he conceded. Another important aspect was the heavy stress on the individual's duties and obligation to serve the 'collective interest' of the community. *Gotong rojong* (mutual assistance and co-operation) was nowhere more a living reality than in the Indonesian village, Sukarno asserted. The village, at least in its utopian conception, offered a whole way of life – a cradle-to-the-grave arrangement – in which, as Weatherbee notes, 'all aspects of the individual's life are regulated through structures and by coercive pressures, formal and informal'. In such a setting, organized opposition is not only out of place, but anti-social. Communal harmony calls for a high level of conformity, and the suppression of individualism. In other words, there is no place in this kind of democracy for student demonstrators, and their like, disturbing the general peace and calm.

In the post-*coup* period, the military has generally

talked of *Pantja Sila* democracy (as opposed to 'liberal democracy' of the fifties and Sukarno's Guided Democracy), but Suharto admitted in October 1970 that the 'form and system of carrying it *(Pantja Sila* democracy) out' was still being sought. At the same time, there is little evidence that the military leaders holding power in Indonesia today opposed Sukarno's idea of Guided Democracy. Indeed, most of them were among those who welcomed his efforts to revive a traditional form of government in preference to the Western-oriented version that had prevailed under the parliament of the fifties. Their real disagreement with Sukarno was over his protection and promotion of the Communist Party, and his neglect of economic issues. Most of the criticism of Sukarno's feudalistic and paternalistic pattern of rule in the post-*coup* period has come from non-Javanese students, civilians and military – not from the Javanese officers now holding the majority of key positions of political and economic power.

There is also little doubt that the more traditional, authoritarian form of democracy offers certain advantages for the military. Its energies have been directed towards ensuring the success of five aims – political and economic stabilization, economic development and reconstruction, the holding of general elections, the prevention of a communist revival and the rehabilitation of the state administrative apparatus. Military leaders generally believe that these objectives can best be pursued in an atmosphere of calm and order. And criticism is only welcome when it has a so-called 'positive' rather than a 'negative' tone. This usually means that criticism and agitation should not be too direct or explicit and not have the effect of lowering the overall reputation of the military or government. And in this regard, it should be noted, Sukarno held similar views concerning criticism discrediting his administration.

During 1970 especially, military intervention in political affairs appeared increasingly to be aimed at silencing opposition and criticism. For instance, the Nationalist

Party under Hadisubeno's leadership is less likely to be publicly critical of government policy than under Hardi. During his campaign for the leadership, Hardi emphasized that while the party would firmly support the government, it should also retain its freedom to speak out critically when this appeared necessary. In contrast, while the party under Hadisubeno's leadership may even be more strongly opposed to some government policy, especially in matters of economics and foreign policy, it is less likely to say so publicly. Similarly, the Indonesian Journalists' Association under Diah's leadership is more likely to be outwardly compliant with the government's wishes than an executive led by Rosihan Anwar.

*

Nonetheless, before jumping to too hasty a conclusion, these developments must also be considered in the light of what has euphemistically been called 'safeguarding' the results of the national elections. During its 1966 session, the Congress decided that 'direct, general, free and secret' elections were to be held by 5 July 1968. The 1968 Congress extended the deadline until 5 July 1971, and until late in 1969, even this date seemed unlikely to be met. But in announcing its intentions to proceed with elections, the government left no one in doubt that they could not be allowed to interfere with political and economic stability. Late in 1969, the deputy commander of KOPKAMTIB, Lieutenant General Sumitro, bluntly declared that the elections were 'not to stir up confusion at all'. Whoever 'plays unfairly', he warned, 'will be destroyed.'

The 'safeguarding' began in parliament. Late in 1969, after nearly three years' laborious debate, the House enacted two bills which virtually ruled out the possibility of significant political change. One dealing with the composition of both Congress and Parliament gave the government a sizeable block of all seats before a single vote was cast. At national level, one-third of a 920-seat Congress and 100 members of a 460-seat Parliament were to be filled by government appointment. At regional level, in provincial and shire legislative chambers, the government share was one-fifth of all seats. Most of these seats were expected to be filled mainly by members of the armed forces. Moreover, the bill dealing with the conduct of the elections contained further provisions that ensured the government should not be embarrassed by the overall results.

Although all citizens aged twenty-one and over (seventeen and over if already married) were technically entitled to vote, important restrictions were included. Explaining that 'it is a democratic right to declare a certain organization which uses force as a means to achieve its goal, and aims at the destruction of democracy itself, to have no right of existence in a democratic state', the election law barred all former members of the outlawed Indonesian Communist Party and its mass organizations, and anyone involved or implicated in the 1965 attempted *coup* from voting. In February 1970, the Minister for Home Affairs, Lieutenant General Amir Machmud, announced that some 2,500 former members of the Masjumi and Socialist Party (PSI) who still harboured 'doubtful intentions' towards the state would also be among those disqualified from taking part in the polls. Other restrictions ruled out independent candidates standing for elections, and stipulated that all candidates would have to meet the approval of the election controllers – a body dominated at all levels by military intelligence and security personnel.

Other 'safeguards' included the further representation of military interest through the Joint Secretariat of Functional Groups (SEKBER GOLKAR). Comprising all the various non-party trade and occupational organizations, this body enjoyed the same rights as the nine political parties authorized to contest the elections, with the added advantage of military backing. [The political parties include the Nationalist Party (PNI), the Religious Scholars League (NU), the Islamic Association Party of Indonesia

(PSII), the Islamic Education Movement (Perti), the Indonesian Muslim Party (Parmusi or PMI), Murba, the Catholic Party, the Christian Party (Parkindo) and League of Upholders of Indonesian Independence (IPKI)]. In some regions, as military personnel moved among potential voters, this allegedly cast doubt upon the freedom voters could expect in exercising their choice. And although the military were technically barred from voting, running for election and campaigning (since they gained direct representation through government appointment), this did not appear to be a great obstacle to their active involvement. If approached either by GOLKAR or a political party to stand as a candidate, a member of the armed forces could obtain 'non-active' status for the period of the campaign. If elected, however, they were required to join the ranks of the civilians.

But political parties were probably hardest hit by the 'safeguards' the government enforced in the regional Houses before polling began. In December 1969, the Minister for Home Affairs, Amir Machmud, issued a regulation for 'purifying' representation of the 'functional groups' (GOLKAR) in the provincial and shire chambers. This was aimed at weeding out all members having any links with political parties. And the regulation stipulated that the regional houses were to have an equal number of representatives from both political parties and functional groups. Moreover, in the case of Houses having odd numbers of members, the majority was to be held by the functional groups. In one blow, this drastically undercut the power of the political parties in the regions, and ensured that no single political party or likely coalition of parties could dominate any of the Houses following the elections. It also meant that the government would retain greater control over the composition of the national Congress, since this body also includes representatives from the regional Houses.

Not surprisingly, many of these measures provoked strong opposition among the political interests most affected, and this may well have had an important bearing on the attitude of the military towards figures such as the Nationalist Party leader, Hardi, and the editor of *Pedoman*, Rosihan Anwar. For instance, Hardi reacted strongly against the regulation 'purifying' the regional Houses. And Rosihan Anwar had persistently attacked Home Affairs Minister Amir Machmud's 'great simplicity of thought', and the way he was implementing the 'government's strategy' or the 'army's strategy' in the forthcoming elections, disregarding 'what the significance of that strategy may be'. Bluntly the paper declared in February 1970: 'In reality, Amir Machmud is acting like a good commandant of troops. The target is clear, that is, he must secure victory for the "government's strategy" in the general elections ... Amir Machmud is a person we have to watch.'

Generally, the attitude of the military has been quite unequivocal. Nothing must be allowed to upset the economic and developmental effort. 'Democracy can be developed only after the general elections,' a senior military official stated frankly in October 1970. 'The important thing now is that development must get priority.'

As a result, political reform has been postponed, perhaps indefinitely. Even though the 1966 Congress directed the government and Parliament to 'immediately draft a bill on the system of parties, mass organizations and functional groups aimed at simplifying them', Suharto has been reluctant to press the issue. Debate on the bill bogged down in endless argument, so that the matter was eventually set aside still unresolved. In a token gesture to political reform, Suharto proposed early in February 1970 that existing parties and functional groups taking part in the elections form themselves into three groups – nationalist, spiritual and functional groups. Although he wanted the merger to take place during the elections, how was not clear, since all parties insisted on maintaining their separate identities for campaigning.

Underlying military reluctance to rock the political

boat is the belief that economic development will bring a 'new atmosphere' under which the kinds of political change needed can be more easily carried out. Suharto talks of the growth of 'sound democracy' as involving the 'awakening of the political consciousness of the people without a repetition of the mistakes of the past'. Among the mistakes he includes 'fanaticism' among political parties and spending resources on prestige projects. Less openly stated, but no less implicit in the military position, is the belief that improved economic conditions among the rural people will undercut the influence of political parties and the noisy political public from which the parties gain their significant support.

But the elections should not be dismissed as a meaningless waste of time and money that might have been better spent on building bridges and repairing roads. In the light of past experience, the need for caution was generally accepted. Few wanted a repetition of the disruptive, divisive 1955 campaign. And despite its 'guides', curbs and restrictions, the 1971 campaign did offer millions of people a much greater sense of participation in government than they had previously enjoyed. Ritual and form have great weight among most Indonesians, so that even elections designed not to seriously disturb the existing political balance, have an intangible worth that should not be too readily discounted. Moreover, this was more than Sukarno ever held, despite his promises. And on a more positive note, the elections should result in a strengthening of the country's deliberative bodies through the infusion of elected representatives for the first time since parliamentary democracy was overthrown in the late fifties.

*

Even so, the voices of the students and other dissenting civilian elements will not be easily stilled. For the most part, the students especially remain restless and sceptical about the future. They do not like the way the Suharto government chooses to rule. They find too much vagueness about its aims and purpose, too much that is temporary and 'stop-gap' about its planning, and too much mystery about the way it often acts.

The students, and their radical civilian supporters, reject the military call for a moratorium on political agitation expressed in slogans like 'economics now, the political game later', asserting that significant economic progress will not be possible without political reform. And in any overhaul of the political system, they especially want a searching examination of cultural values and attitudes that are often found among the 'buried treasure' from the past. They argue that from such an inquiry will emerge the main reasons for the country's continued backwardness and uncertain future.

For much the same reason, the students strongly attack the military for forming an alliance with rural-based Central and East Javanese elements of the Nationalist Party. They point out that the leaders of these same elements are among the foremost opponents of the government's economic and foreign policies. And they fear that through seeking the support of those who refrain from open criticism of corruption and other deviations while silencing other criticism (such as from the students themselves), the government will 'rot from within'. At the same time, they observe the military continually consolidating and extending its own powers and privileges, and they fear that it may become too engrossed in defending these to pursue overall national interests.

The students also defend their often unruly behaviour in traditional terms. In replying to criticism of their 'un-Oriental' behaviour, they argue that, in fact, Javanese culture has a place for rude and disrespectful behaviour which has the function of 'social renewal'. They refer to the cruder figures of classical Javanese art, asserting that these had the task of giving vent to the people's frustrations and drawing attention to society's shortcomings. Nor should those in authority show irritation and impatience with such behaviour since, according to Javanese custom, that was the reaction only of authorities who felt they were in the wrong. And as examples of eminent Indonesians who have brought about reform and mobilized society's potentials, by their forthright and unconventional behaviour they mention, among others, the famous fourteenth century Prime Minister, Gadjah Mada, who is credited with having been the driving force behind the Madjapahit empire, as well as – ironically – Sukarno, and Jakarta's post-*coup* governor, Ali Sadikin.

While Sukarno generally reserved his unconventional behaviour for dealings with the outside world and domestic rivals (and these were not traditional Javanese), and Ali Sadikin is a Sundanese from West Java, the students still have a point. Despite the military's claims to being a modernizing and dynamizing force in society, it has yet to provide convincing proof to support such claims. Too often military leaders can be found hiding behind the skirts of traditional authority, which does not accept being questioned by those of lesser rank. And for the young students especially, who have only contempt for the old party politicians, it is a central cause for concern that they should find the army leadership still basically conservative and traditional in outlook.

But among the handful of military leaders who have shown a refreshing balance between the demands of development and respect for the treasures of the past, few have attracted more attention than Major General (Marines) Ali Sadikin. Appointed governor of Jakarta in 1966, he immediately set about transforming its dusty, rutted roads, rundown transport system and seedy, paint-shy buildings into a city that could be some cause for pride among its $4\frac{1}{2}$ million inhabitants.

As an organizer, Ali Sadikin is energetic and impatient with those who want to engage in endless planning and discussion. 'There's been too much talking for years,' he told me once during an interview. 'Talking, talking, talking ... We all know the problems and what has to be done. What we need now is to find the money and get on with the job.' His methods of finding funds – lotteries, casinos and risqué entertainment for the rich – brought him into sharp conflict with religious and cultural watch-dogs, but he silenced most of his critics with results.

With Ali Sadikin as governor, city roads are repaired twelve months of the year and not just during the 'dry season'. Clean, serviceable buses are also back on the streets (and they run to schedules). And in one sixteen month period, his administration built more new schools than during the previous sixteen years. He has also become a vigorous patron of the arts – not by dominating and dic-tating to the city's intellectual and artistic community as was Sukarno's way – but by providing funds, facilities and encouragement, and leaving the rest to the initiative of the artists themselves. 'I am trying to preserve our national identity,' he argues. 'But it's difficult to say just what that is. And it changes with time.' As a result, Ali Sadikin is a hero among students. 'He is a modernist,' they assert approvingly. 'He confronts facts with an open mind ... is critical of prejudice and taboos.'

But the dissenters are also not without blame. Both the students and other civilians could do much more to pre-serve the rights and opportunities they claim the military are eroding. In the regions especially, civilians often volun-tarily abdicate jobs they accuse the military of usurping because they are afraid of accepting responsibility. 'If there is trouble,' the commander of the East Indonesia Territorial Defence Command, Lieutenant General Kemal Idris, declared in June 1970, 'the military is always asked to intervene. And even to cut the ribbon at an opening ceremony, everyone wants the military. If there is an issue of militarism, it is the civilians themselves who are to blame because they are not ready for their tasks. They fear responsibility.'

The students also have often fallen short of the ideals they espouse. After Sukarno's overthrow, they quickly disintegrated into squabbling factions, reflecting their own lack of purpose, discipline and clearly defined aims.

In October 1969, the fourth anniversary of the foundation of the KAMI, once the most powerful of all 'action fronts', a Jakarta daily wrote despairingly: 'Today KAMI is just a name. It no longer has an impact on society.' And in a mood of introspection in July 1970, the student paper *Harian KAMI* blamed rivalry and self-interest among student leaders as the main reasons for the failure of student power. 'Idealists with character are scarce now,' the paper bemoaned. In their divided and disorganized state, the students still retain a degree of influence during their periodic outbursts against corruption and the military's abuse of 'civil rights' but they can usually be fairly quickly neutralized and silenced by astute government pressure.

And as to future conflict between traditional forces and those pressing for change – and the debate and disagreement this entails on issues such as democracy, the right to dissent, and the need for social values and attitudes that are in tune with the demands of development and the twentieth century – some headway might be made during the seventies if a suggestion made by one Jakarta daily in October 1970 was put into practice. 'It may do us some good in talking about society's problems to forget for a while such terms and phrases as *Pantja Sila*, the armed forces' "dual function", "civil rights", "rule of law", "justice and truth" and so on. They are worn out and meaningless because of the way they are used to suit a particular interest's arguments or as a means of quietening an opponent.' The paper also suggested a moratorium on phrases like 'in the interests of the people', 'for the sake of Indonesia's genuine and characteristic culture' and 'for the sake of our country's glory'. 'By deliberately avoiding them,' the daily added, 'we will encourage fresh and new thinking and ward off rigid stands and views which often encumber co-operation and efforts at cultivating mutual understanding among the various groups in our society.'

But if the conflict leads to rising tensions as dissident elements press their demands, there is little doubt that military leaders are prepared to get much tougher. In his Armed Forces' day address on 5 October 1970, Suharto declared that the military did not intend being a 'fire brigade' that went away as soon as the fire was put out. Pressure, he warned, aimed at the military 'can arouse feelings among the military favouring undemocratic steps.' Another senior army officer told me in 1969: 'Our job is only to help. But if everything goes wrong, we can take over and we *will* take over. But only when the situation is hopeless.'

Bibliography

ADAMS, CINDY *My Friend the Dictator*, New York, Bobbs-Merrill, 1967.

ANDERSON, B. R. O'G. *Mythology and the Tolerance of the Javanese*, Ithaca, N.Y., Cornell University Modern Indonesia Project, 1965.

BASTIN, J. and BENDA, H. J. *A History of Modern Southeast Asia, Colonialism, Nationalism and Decolonization*, Englewood Cliffs, N.J., Prentice-Hall, 1968.

BRACKMAN, ARNOLD C. *The Communist Collapse in Indonesia*, New York, W. W. Norton & Co., 1969.

DAHM, BERNHARD *Sukarno and the Struggle for Indonesian Independence*, Ithaca, N.Y., Cornell University Press, 1969.

FEITH, HERBERT *The Decline of Constitutional Democracy in Indonesia*, Ithaca, N.Y., Cornell University Press, 1962.

FEITH, HERBERT 'Suharto's Search for a Political Format', *Australia's Neighbours*, (Melbourne) May-June, 1968.

FEITH, HERBERT & CASTLES, LANCE (Eds.) *Indonesian Political Thinking 1945-1965*, Ithaca, N.Y., Cornell University Press, 1970.

GEERTZ, CLIFFORD *The Religion of Java*, London, Collier-Macmillan, 1960.

GRANT, BRUCE *Indonesia*, Melbourne, Melbourne University Press, revised 1967.

GULICK, SIDNEY LEWIS *The East and The West*, Rutland, Vermont, Charles E. Tuttle Co., 1963.

HALL, D. G. E. *A History of Southeast Asia*, London, Macmillan, 1964.

HANNA, WILLARD A. 'The Magical-Mystical Syndrome in the Indonesian Mentality', *American Universities Field*

Staff Reports Service, Southeast Asia Series, vol. 15, nos. 5–8 (Indonesia).

HINDLEY, DONALD *The Communist Party of Indonesia 1951-1963*, Berkeley & Los Angeles, University of California Press, 1964.

HINDLEY, DONALD 'Dilemmas of Consensus and Divisions: Indonesia's Search for a Political Format', *Government and Opposition*, (London), Winter 1969.

HUGHES, JOHN *Indonesian Upheaval*, New York, McKay, 1967.

JAY, ROBERT R. *Religion and Politics in Rural Central Java*, Cultural Report Series no. 12, Southeast Asia Studies, Yale University, 1963.

KAHIN, GEORGE MCTURNAN *Nationalism and Revolution in Indonesia*, Ithaca, N.Y., Cornell University Press, 1952.

KROEF, J. M. van der, *The Communist Party of Indonesia, Its History, Program and Tactics*, Vancouver, University of British Columbia, 1965.

KROEF, J. M. van der, 'Indonesian Communism Since the 1965 Coup', *Pacific Affairs*, Spring 1970.

LEGGE, J. D. *Indonesia*, Englewood Cliffs, N.Y., Prentice-Hall, 1965.

LEGGE, J. D. 'General Suharto's New Order', *International Affairs*, January 1968.

LEV, DANIEL S. *The Transition to Guided Democracy: Indonesian Politics 1957-1959,* Ithaca, N.Y., Cornell University Modern Indonesia Project, 1966.

LEV, DANIEL S. 'Indonesia: The Year of the Coup', *Asian Survey*, February 1966.

'LUCIEN REY' 'Dossier of the Indonesian Drama', *New Left Review*, March-April 1966.

MCVEY, RUTH T. (Ed.) *Indonesia*, New Haven, HRAF Press, 1963.

MCVEY, RUTH T. 'Indonesian Communism and China', in Tang Tsou, Ed., *China in Crisis*, vol. 2, Chicago, University of Chicago Press, 1968.

MALIK, ADAM 'Promise in Indonesia', *Foreign Affairs*, January, 1968.

MOZENGO, DAVID P. 'China's Policy Towards Indonesia', in Tang Tsou, Ed., *China in Crisis*, vol. 2, Chicago, University of Chicago Press, 1968.

NASUTION, A. H. *Fundamentals of Guerrilla Warfare*, London, Pall Mall 1965.

NUGROHO *Indonesia: Facts and Figures*, Jakarta, Pertjobaan, 1967.

NUGROHO NOTOSUSANTO and ISMAEL SALEH *The Coup Attempt of the September 30 Movement in Indonesia*, Jakarta, P. T. Pembimbing Masa, 1968.

PAGET, ROGER 'The Military in Indonesian Politics: The Burden of Power', *Pacific Affairs*, Fall-Winter, 1967.

PAUKER, GUY J. 'Indonesia in 1966: The Year of Transition', *Asian Survey*, February 1967.

PAUKER, GUY J. 'Towards a New Order in Indonesia', *Foreign Affairs*, April 1967.

PENNY, DAVID H. 'The Economics of Peasant Agriculture: The Indonesian Case', *Bulletin of Indonesian Economic Studies* (Australian National University, Canberra), October 1966.

PURCELL, VICTOR *The Chinese in Southeast Asia*, London, Oxford University Press, 1965.

ROEDER, O. G. *The Smiling General*, Jakarta, Gunung Agung, 1969.

SHAPLEN, ROBERT *Time Out of Hand: Revolution and Reaction in Southeast Asia*, New York, Harper & Row, 1969.

SJAHRIR, SUTAN *Out of Exile*, New York, John Day, 1949.

SUDJATMOKO 'Indonesia: Problems and Opportunities', *Australian Outlook*, December 1967.

SUKARNO *An Autobiography*, as told to Cindy Adams, New York, Bobbs-Merrill, 1965.

SUMITRO DJOJOHADIKUSUMO 'Indonesia Disenchanted?', *New Guinea*, October 1967.

SUNDHAUSSEN, ULF *The Soldier and the Nation: The Self-Perception of the Indonesian Army and its Role in Politics*, Monash University, November 1970 (for a German translation, *Europa-Archiv*, 16 March 1971).

TAKDIR ALISJAHBANA, S. *Indonesia: Social and Cultural Revolution*, Kuala Lumpur, Oxford University Press, 1966.

VLEKKE, BERNHARD H. M. *Nusantara: A History of Indonesia*, The Hague and Bandung, Van Hoeve Ltd, 1959.

WAGNER, FRITS A. *The Art of Indonesia*, New York, Crown, 1959.

WERTHEIM, W. F. *Indonesian Society in Transition*, The Hague and Bandung, Van Hoeve Ltd, 1959.

WERTHEIM, W. F. 'Indonesia Before and After the Untung Coup', *Pacific Affairs*, Spring-Summer 1966.

WILLNER, ANN RUTH *The Neotraditional Accommodation to Political Independence: The Case of Indonesia* Princeton University Centre of International Studies, 1966.

Index

Index

Index

Index

Index